W9-BUG-324

FERGUSON
CAREER BIOGRAPHIES

GLORIA
ESTEFAN

Singer

James Robert Parish

Ferguson
An imprint of Infobase Publishing

Gloria Estefan: Singer

Copyright © 2006 by Infobase Publishing

Ferguson
An imprint of Infobase Publishing
132 West 31st Street
New York NY 10001

Parish, James Robert.
   Gloria Estefan : singer / James Robert Parish.
      p. cm.
   Includes index.
   ISBN 0-8160-5833-4 (hc : alk. paper)
   1. Estefan, Gloria. 2. Singers—United States—Biography. 3. Singing—Instruction and study. I. Title.
   ML420.E87.P37 2006
   782.42164092—dc22   2005033992

Text design by David Strelecky

Pages 93–111 adapted from Ferguson's *Encyclopedia of Careers and Vocational Guidance, Thirteenth Edition*

Printed in the United States of America

MP FOF 10 9 8 7 6 5 4 3 2 1

This book is printed on acid-free paper.

CONTENTS

1

THE QUEEN OF LATIN POP

One of Gloria Estefan's guiding philosophies is, "You never know what life has in store for you, but I believe there are certain things one is meant to go through."

On the snowy morning of March 20, 1990, Gloria Estefan's tour bus was traveling along an icy highway in eastern Pennsylvania, near Scranton. The previous day Gloria, accompanied by her husband, musician/recording industry entrepreneur Emilio Estefan Jr., and their 12-year-old son, Nayib, had been in Washington, D.C. They had met with President George Bush at the White House to discuss the singer's participation in the president's ongoing "War Against Drugs" program. Now Gloria, her immediate family, two tour staff members, and Nayib's tutor were heading to a concert engagement in Syracuse, New York. Long afraid of flying, Gloria was glad to be traveling in her customized vehicle. She reasoned, "I love the bus. If you crash, at least you're not falling 37,000 feet."

As the bus proceeded along Interstate 380 they came upon a road accident. A tractor-trailer had jackknifed and was now blocking the highway. The driver of Estefan's vehicle made a sudden but safe stop. At the time, Gloria had been resting on the bus's built-in couch. She awoke and looked out the window, observing the falling snow and the peaceful countryside. Behind the singer's bus, a semi-trailer truck was fast approaching. The driver of the rig was unable to apply his brakes in time, and the huge truck crashed into Gloria's bus. The mighty force of the collision pushed the bus into the disabled truck ahead. At the time of this accident, the singer was still lying down resting. Her son was in the back of the bus going over his daily school lessons with his tutor. Her husband, Emilio, was up front by the bus's stairwell taking care of some business.

The strong impact of the collision propelled Gloria onto the floor. As she recalled, "I felt disconnected from my body, and there was excruciating pain when I tried to move my legs and feet." Meanwhile, in the back of the bus, Nayib and his instructor were buried beneath a pile of suitcases, clothing, and other items. Emilio, who now had a badly cut hand, moved toward his wife who was lying relatively motionless but conscious. In shock and in denial, he tried to reassure her, insisting, "It's okay. You just pulled a muscle." (However, Gloria, who felt a strange electric taste in her mouth, knew that her injuries were far more serious.) Despite her agonizing pain, the singing star's only concern was the welfare of their son.

Bleeding and dazed, Mr. Estefan crawled to the back of the bus and dug through the debris. Soon he had unburied his son and the female tutor. The boy's shoulder ached badly, but he was otherwise relatively okay. (Later it was discovered that the teenager had broken his collarbone.) When Gloria learned that her son

Cuban-born singer Gloria Estefan waves to fans during a performance in Rockefeller Center. (Associated Press)

was alive and mobile, she sighed with great relief. Later she recalled, "With Nayib and Emilio alive, I knew that I could manage whatever else might happen."

Realizing that she must not move until medical attention arrived, Gloria lay in extreme agony as her husband, son, and the others aboard (who had relatively minor injuries) tried to comfort her. Despite her growing inner terror, the celebrated vocalist did not cry out, but kept the pain within. "I was forced to really keep a lot of control, because I didn't want Nayib freaking out." To reassure her frightened son, she kept hold of his hand.

In the midst of her anguish, the singer suddenly understood a decision she had made three years earlier. At the time, 1987, the Estefans were remodeling a large house near Miami Beach. Although Estefan was then in perfect health, she had insisted that the contractors install an elevator in the magnificent two-story home. She had a premonition that, one day, she would need it because she would be disabled. (Some of Gloria's concern was based on the fact that her late father had spent the last 12 years of his life confined to bed because of an ailment similar to multiple sclerosis.) Gripped with fear as she lay in the crushed bus, Estefan told herself, "My God, it's happened. The thing that I . . . always feared most."

A Fateful Decision

Because of perilous road conditions and the stalled traffic along the Interstate, it took well over an hour for the Scranton Community Medical Center ambulance to reach the accident site. Once there, the doctors needed to determine the extent of her physical damage. As Estefan remembers, "The pain was almost unbearable as I was strapped to a board and carried through the hole that used to be the windshield. I could feel the snow on my face and the people looking down at me with fear in their eyes."

After careful assessment at the hospital, the doctors confirmed what Gloria had suspected. She had fractured two vertebrae. Her back was broken. When Emilio heard the devastating news, he fainted. Meanwhile, the singer coped with the overwhelming medical diagnosis. Gloria dreaded the idea of being dependent on others like her father had been during his illness.

The doctors offered Gloria two options of treatment. One involved several months of being in a cast to mend her broken body. She would emerge unparalyzed, but would, most likely, not have full use of her limbs. The other choice was a fairly new treatment in which surgeons would place two permanent eight-inch rods in her back to support her injured spinal cord. The physicians warned that the innovative surgery was risky; if she should develop even a simple infection, she might end up paralyzed for life. On the other hand, if the operation was successful, she would be able to resume her performing career.

It did not take Gloria long to make her decision to undergo this surgery. On March 21, with Emilio at her side, she was flown by medical helicopter to the Orthopedic Institute Hospital for Joint Diseases in New York City, an institution that specialized in the new medical procedure. There the famous patient underwent a grueling four-hour operation. The surgical team inserted the two steel rods in the patient and fused together her spine with ground bits of

Gloria, with her son, Nayib, beside her, arrives in Miami several days after her near-fatal 1990 bus accident. (Associated Press)

her broken vertebrae. It required over 400 stitches to close the 14-inch incision in her back. By the time that Gloria was in the recovery room, Emilio had been told by the surgeons that his wife would regain anywhere from 95 to 100 percent of her past mobility.

An intensive, highly painful convalescent period started, but within several months Gloria made tremendous progress in her near-miraculous recovery. She continued to work hard in her rehabilitation program. To everyone's amazement, Estefan was by the following year once again on stage performing energetically for her fans.

A Big Life Lesson

Gloria Estefan learned much from her terrifying accident. Now she fully appreciated that "You can't just let life land on you. Bad things happen, of course, but you have to take control of your life." She admitted, "Learning to walk again was the most difficult. But I learned not to take things for granted and to enjoy every second now. I'd always had my priorities straight, but when you almost lose everything it really sets you straight."

Thereafter, the "Queen of Latin Pop" would make a series of new, best-selling albums. These award-winning releases confirmed her status as a Latina artist who had achieved tremendous mainstream success. Gloria, who had overcome so many obstacles and tragedies in her life, emerged from her road accident a bigger icon than ever. She had proven anew to be a glowing example to all those who have the determination and courage to follow their career dreams and life's goals—no matter what.

2

MIAMI LIFE

Gloria Maria Milagrosa Fajardo was born on September 1, 1957, in Havana, Cuba. She was the first of two daughters of José Manuel Fajardo and his wife, Gloria (Garcia) Fajardo. In his youth, the father had been a bronze medal–winning volleyball player at the Pan American Games. Now he was a member of the police security squad assigned as driver and bodyguard to protect the family of Cuba's president, General Fulgencio Batista (1901–73). Her mother was a credentialed schoolteacher.

Noted for its production of sugar, tobacco, and seafood, Cuba is the largest and westernmost of the islands of the West Indies. It is located at the mouth of the Gulf of Mexico. In 1492 explorer Christopher Columbus had claimed Cuba as a Spanish colony. Although the island country obtained its freedom from Spain in 1898, it quickly came under strong U.S. influence and control. In 1934 Cuba finally became self-governing. Six years later, during one of many local political upheavals, Batista, a soldier and statesman, became the country's president. In 1944, Batista's tight-fisted regime lost control of Cuba. However, he returned to power in 1952.

Batista's government—well known for its ruthlessness and corruption—favored the rich and did little to help the country's many poor inhabitants. This situation prompted socialist revolutionaries led by Fidel Castro, with the help of Ernesto "Che" Guevara and many others, to bring down Batista's rule in early 1959 and to take control of Cuba. With Batista forced into exile, Castro set up a communist regime and punished many of the general's followers.

In this new political climate it was no longer safe for José Fajardo and his family to remain in Cuba. Like thousands of others who opposed the new government under Castro, the Fajardos had to leave their homeland. Already watched by Castro's forces, the Fajardos fled to Miami, some 90 miles north across the waters aboard a Pan American jet. (To avoid suspicion, the family purchased round-trip fares, making it seem as if they planned to return to Havana in the near future. To this day, Gloria still has her return ticket, a memory of a most painful time in her life.)

Along with many other refugees who had fled with few belongings or money, the Fajardos moved into a ghetto near Miami's Orange Bowl stadium. Having been a member of Cuba's middle class who lived fairly well in

Havana, life in Miami was a tremendous adjustment for the family. They often had no beds in which to sleep nor any proper cooking utensils. For a time they survived on charity, living on meager rations of cheese, Spam, and drinks obtained at the local-based Freedom Tower, a distribution point in Miami for the exiles. Eventually, they settled into one of the rundown, barracks-style apartment buildings inhabited by Cuban refugees of the time.

Adding to their problems, the displaced Cubans faced a great deal of discrimination from the Florida locals. Gloria recalls vividly, "In Miami there was a lot of prejudice at the time. It was very difficult . . . all these Hispanics coming into one place that had never had any Hispanics at all. I remember that my mom had a really tough time dealing with [the bigotry]."

A Secret Mission

With no money coming in and longing to return with his family to their homeland, José joined with many of his fellow countrymen to work secretly with the Central Intelligence Agency (CIA). The CIA, a U.S. government agency dealing with espionage overseas, was secretly plotting with Cuban expatriates to stage a takeover in Cuba. The CIA hoped to use this scheme to remove Castro's regime from power because it had become too closely allied with the Soviet Union, a major communist power.

This was the era of the Cold War, in which there was high tension among world powers—especially between the Soviet Union and the United States. The U.S. was greatly concerned that the Soviets were placing missile bases on Cuba, threatening the safety of mainland America.

In the spring of 1961, a few months after John F. Kennedy was elected president, the CIA arranged an unofficial invasion of Cuba. The CIA provided weapons, supplies, and money to 1,300 Cubans who would travel by boat and land on the beach at Cuba's Bay of Pigs. It was assumed that the Cuban locals would join with the invaders in the overthrow of Castro's forces.

In preparation for this dangerous mission, José Fajardo left Miami to train in secret, sending money to his family in his absence. During this period Mrs. Fajardo was confused and frightened by her husband's undisclosed activities, especially when she received a brief note from her husband telling her that he was going off to help free their country. He did not say exactly where he was going.

On April 17, 1961 the invasion of the Bay of Pigs took place. It proved to be a resounding failure, as Castro's forces were ready and waiting for the attackers. The small task force (the 2506 Brigade) received none of the support promised by the CIA. At the last minute President Kennedy, realizing that the campaign was going badly, refused to send American military forces—including air support—to help the Cuban rebels. Adding to the fiasco, none of the expected support from Cubans on the island was forthcoming.

The botched CIA mission resulted in the death or capture of many of the Cuban freedom fighters at the Bay of Pigs. José, who headed a small tank division, was taken prisoner and put in prison. Gloria's mother, not wanting to scare her little girl, refused to admit to her child that José was in jail. She just said he was away for the time being. Young Gloria learned the truth about her dad's whereabouts from overhearing discussions among her neighbors.

Initially, the CIA denied any participation in the failed operation. Later, President Kennedy made a TV appearance in which he and his administration took full responsibility for the military and political disaster. Eventually, a few days before Christmas of 1962, a deal was made with Castro's government that the U.S. would provide Cuba with $53 million of food and medical supplies in exchange for the release of the surviving members of the task force.

Not long after José Fajardo was reunited with his family in Miami, he joined the U.S. Army, hoping that one day America would back another invasion attempt on Cuba. As part of the American military—in which he eventually rose to the rank of captain—Fajardo and his family were

Gloria's father, like the Cuban men pictured here, was captured and imprisoned after the failed U.S.-led Bay of Pigs invasion in 1961. (Getty Images)

stationed at a series of military bases, including Lackland Air Force Base near San Antonio, Texas. These relocations meant that young Gloria, then in the first grade and just learning to speak English (rather than her native Spanish), was constantly being uprooted. During this period the Fajardos' second child, Rebecca, was born.

A New Influence

In her first-grade classroom in San Antonio, Gloria came into contact with a wonderful mentor: her teacher Dorothy Collins. Gloria describes this important individual: "She's African-American and she was the most influential person in my life. To this day, she still stays in touch with me through my mother. At the time, I was the only Hispanic in her class. I started first grade without knowing how to read English. But she really worked with me, and after six months, I won a prize [for reading skills]. It was very controversial, because all these other mothers couldn't believe it. But Mrs. Collins stuck by me and said I deserved the honor."

Some months later, José Fajardo was restationed to Fort Jackson in Columbia, South Carolina. Because he (and his family) would be based there for at least two years, Gloria begged that as they now had a "permanent" home, that she should be allowed to have a pet. After much pleading her mother agreed that if she earned straight A's on her report card, she would consider allowing her older child to get a dog. According to Gloria, "I've always loved a challenge and came through on my part of the bargain. This is where my favorite childhood memory was born. We drove out to a farm where one of my dad's friends had a litter of German shepherd puppies. I knelt down on the ground, and one of the chubby furry little pups ran right into my arms." Named Dolly, the canine became the youngster's "best friend for years to come!"

Daddy's Girl

In 1966 U.S. soldier José Fajardo was ordered to duty in Vietnam. At the time America was involved in a quickly escalating civil war between South (pro-U.S.) and North (pro-communist) Vietnam. Missing her father greatly, little Gloria would often record songs for her dad on the tapes that she sent to him. José wrote back that he was sure that one day his gifted daughter would become a singing star.

Already music had become an important part of Gloria's young life. She recalled, "Specific events, sights and even smells are forever linked to the songs that I heard playing at that time." For example, one day she and her mother were going to the local laundromat. On the car radio a song ("Ferry Across the Mersey") sung by the British rock group Gerry and the Pacemakers was playing. Fascinated by this mild rock-and-roll number, the youngster refused to leave the car until the melody was over. Said Estefan, 'I didn't know what a ferry was, let alone the Mersey, but there was such longing in that song, it really reached me. Whenever I hear that song, I can still smell the laundromat."

Actually, the love of music was inborn in Gloria. Her mother had enjoyed singing as a child, once winning a big contest by duplicating the vocalizing skills of young Hollywood movie star Shirley Temple. Then too, among Gloria's relatives there had been a salsa pianist, a classical violinist, and two amateur singer/songwriters.

In September 1966, while José Fajardo was still serving in Vietnam, Mrs. Fajardo bought Gloria a guitar for her ninth birthday. It was an instrument that a family friend had brought back from Spain, the homeland of Gloria's grandparents. Mrs. Fajardo had the girl take lessons to play classical guitar. Gloria quickly found the instruction boring and felt it took away from the pleasure she got from learning to play the guitar on her own. Nevertheless, at her mother's insistence she kept up with the training for a while. Soon she learned to pick out melodies of her own creation, often playing by ear as she listened to the radio.

By 1968, José Fajardo was back from Vietnam and the family was reunited in Miami. Sadly, their rejoicing was short lived. Not long after returning from overseas, José began having physical and mental problems. For example, he was not able to distinguish between green and red traffic lights, and often when driving would stop on green signals. He also began having difficulty walking and would sometimes fall down. Physicians diagnosed him as suffering from a form of multiple sclerosis. (This is a serious type of progressive disease of the central nervous system that leads to the victim becoming weak and not being able to control the body's muscles. This illness is believed to be triggered by a malfunction of the immune system.)

Other doctors who studied Fajardo's medical case believed that José was one of the thousands of soldiers who had served in Vietnam who were victims of Agent Orange. During the war, U.S. forces had sprayed a chemical—known as Agent Orange—on the jungle turf. This toxic spray was designed to kill much of the vegetation used by the enemy to hide and to ambush American troops. Unfortunately, Agent Orange had a severe impact on the health of many Vietnamese and U.S. soldiers who were exposed to it.

Before long, Gloria's ailing father was bedridden. With little pension money forthcoming from his military service, Gloria's mother had to go out to work. She found a day job and took classes at night to improve her English and teaching skills and become certified to teach elementary school in the U.S. Meanwhile, while Gloria was herself in the classroom, Mrs. Fajardo found someone to watch José and little Rebecca. But when 11-year-old Gloria came home from school, it was then up to her to take care of her invalid father and her little sister.

The tremendous pressure of dealing with so many responsibilities was a terrible burden for Gloria. She remembers, "I looked so much older than I do now because

I was carrying the weight of the whole world on my shoulders." However, she refused to show her unhappiness or talk about the responsibilities given her. She felt it was her duty to make things as easy as possible for the others at home and especially Mrs. Fajardo who had to spend so much time away from the family. Gloria admitted later, "I would not cry. I was afraid if I let go just a little bit it would all go." The overwhelming situation left the adolescent struggling to maintain her emotional balance. "I had very dark thoughts. It was a situation that had no solution. But it was good because it made me very strong. When you're a kid you think that nothing is ever going to change. . . . I thought, my God, this is going to be my life forever."

During this troublesome time, music became increasingly important in the girl's life. According to Gloria, "Music was my escape. It was my release from everything. I'd lock myself up in my room with my guitar. . . . I would sing for hours by myself." In the privacy of her hideaway, she would write lyrics about the emotional pains of her life and then sing the songs to herself. Sometimes the process would make her start to cry, allowing her bottled-up feelings to come out. Such emotional release helped the teenager cope with watching over her little sister, caring for her increasingly ill dad (who was embarrassed and humiliated to be dependent upon his older girl), and being strong on the surface to keep up her mom's spirits.

Sometimes, to divert her family, the girl would sing for them, often harmonizing with her cousin, Mercedes "Merci" Navarro. Other times, when Gloria was by herself, she would sing the Cuban songs her mother and grandmother (who also lived in Miami) had taught her. On other occasions, she would vocalize to songs playing on the radio. For Gloria, "Music was the one bright spot in my life."

Among Gloria's favorite performers of this time were such Hispanic ballad singers as Agustín Lara and Jorge Negrete, and such American vocalists as Karen Carpenter, Johnny Mathis, Barbra Streisand, and Diana Ross. Another of her favorite artists was singer/songwriter Carole King. Gloria was especially affected by King's 1971 pop album *Tapestry*, an emotionally expressive and intimate album (with such songs as "I Feel the Earth Move," "It's Too Late," and "(You Make Me Feel Like) A Natural Woman." The teenager describes *Tapestry* as "one of the most influential albums, as a total album, in my life."

Household Changes

By the time Gloria was 16, Mr. Fajardo's health had worsened. Finally, needing full-time professional care, he was relocated to a local Veteran's Administration hospital where his condition continued to deteriorate.

The new situation allowed Gloria more time for herself. However, much of the responsibility for running the household was still upon her, as Mrs. Fajardo was teaching at a public school. The adolescent had the constant strain of trying to boost family morale while coping with her dad's plight. She often visited him at the hospital. He remained bedridden, often did not remember his loved ones, and could scarcely talk. The girl would leave such visits feeling extremely sad. (She recalls that it reached the point where "you pray that the suffering will end, because you can't imagine why anyone has to go through something like that.")

When Gloria entered Our Lady of Lourdes Academy, an all-girls Roman Catholic junior-high and high school in South Miami, she was a respectful, quiet pupil who studied hard and earned good grades.

The Gloria of this period wore glasses, was overweight, and quite shy in social situations. Unlike her peers, she never dated. Occasionally bashful Gloria would be asked to entertain fellow students by singing in school talent shows. She did so timidly, but for a few minutes she came out of her shell. Eventually, the nuns at Our Lady of Lourdes became convinced that solemn and quiet Gloria would one day become a nun herself.

In actuality the teenager had no such ambitions. Graduating from high school in 1975, Gloria planned on attending college. She thought of perhaps becoming a teacher or a psychologist.

3

A SINGER IS BORN

During the summer of 1975 before 17-year-old Gloria began college, she had the opportunity to be a typical teenager. She spent more quality time with her friends and made new acquaintances. She and some of her girlfriends (including cousin Merci Navarro) formed an amateur singing group. They rehearsed often and even performed at a party or two.

The father of one of her friends knew a professional musician who was the head of a local band, the Miami Latin Boys. He asked the musician to give Gloria's teen vocal group a few pointers about singing. The young man agreed to meet with the girls. At the appointed time, 22-year-old Emilio Estefan Jr. arrived for the session. Gloria describes, "He came over with his accordion and these little short shorts, and I thought he was cute."

Gloria and Emilio Estefan in 2004 (Landov)

A Dynamic New Friend

Emilio Estefan Jr. was born on March 4, 1953, in Lebanon. While he was still young, his family moved to Cuba. As a child Emilio displayed a great interest in music, although no other relatives were musically inclined. The bright youngster begged to have an accordion, which he taught himself to play. After Fidel Castro took control of Cuba in 1959, the family remained in the country, hoping somehow to keep control of the factory they owned. By the mid-1960s it became clear that the island's communist government would soon take over the family business, as it had done with many other companies. The Estefans felt their only option was to leave Cuba. However, because the family's older son, José, was of draft age, he was not allowed to depart the country. Reluctantly, Mr. Estefan and 13-year-old Emilio left their adopted homeland, hoping, somehow, that in the future Mrs. Estefan and José could join them

Emilio and his father first went to Spain, where they spent two years trying to gain legal entry into the U.S. Eventually, their efforts succeeded, and in 1967 they emigrated to Miami, Florida. There, for a time, they lived in cramped quarters with 15 other relatives. Initially, young Emilio knew no English, making it tough for him to adjust at school. After classes, the enterprising young man found odd jobs in his neighborhood, such as doing errands for the elderly, selling T-shirts and other items, and even staging local beauty competitions. Later the teenager became a mail clerk for Bacardi Imports Inc., a company that specialized in distilling rum made from sugarcane grown on many of the Caribbean islands. The hard-working newcomer was soon promoted at Bacardi. Eventually, years later, he would be placed in charge of the firm's marketing in Latin America.

While the ambitious Emilio thrived at his various positions at Bacardi, he was still far more intrigued with performing music. On many evenings and on weekends he joyfully played his accordion at local restaurants for tips. One day Estefan's supervisor at Bacardi learned that his employee was a musician. He offered the young man an opportunity to play for pay at an upcoming private party. Because the host wished to have dancing at the festivities, he asked Emilio to bring along a drummer and additional musicians. Estefan's music teacher recommended two candidates: 17-year-old drummer Enrique "Kiki" Garcia and 15-year-old bass player Juan Marcos Avila. The group's performance was a success and their pleased host gave this newly formed band a name: Miami Latin Boys. Subsequently, the group played several more local gigs and developed a positive reputation in Miami's Cuban community. The group soon boasted nine instrumentalists.

Joining the Band

Three months after Gloria first encountered Emilio Estefan, she and her mother were invited to a friend's wedding. At the time Gloria was just starting classes at the University of Miami and had found a job at Miami International Airport as a part-time translator for the U.S. Customs Service. Busy with her many activities, the 18-year old did not want to go to the wedding. Mrs. Fajardo had to drag her reluctant daughter to the occasion.

Once at the festivities Gloria discovered that the band playing was the Miami Latin Boys. It was not long before Emilio recognized Gloria among the guests. He suggested that she join his group on stage to sing a few numbers. She was hesitant, but her mother and others persuaded her to do so. She sang two old Cuban standards. When she finished performing in her warm, sincere style, the audience applauded enthusiastically. The positive response surprised modest Gloria, but she thought little more about her brief taste of success as an entertainer.

However, it was not long before an idea sprung into Emilio's mind. None of the many bands that had sprung up in the city used a female vocalist. To make the Miami Latin Boys stand out from their rivals, Estefan asked Gloria to join his talented group. Initially, she said no. She was too busy with college and her job as a translator. Not discouraged, Emilio pursued the idea with the young woman. To persuade her to say yes, he said that he would arrange the schedule so that she only had to sing on weekends. To help her decide in his favor, he invited Gloria and her relatives to come and watch the band play and to meet his family.

Increasingly drawn to this charismatic, handsome man, Gloria finally agreed to the offer. There was still one more obstacle. While Mrs. Fajardo had not minded her daughter singing occasionally at friends' parties, she worried about her girl rehearsing and working unchaperoned among a group of young male musicians. Finally, it was decided that if Gloria's cousin, Merci Navarro (who was very serious about a professional singing career), was allowed to join Emilio's group, it would be okay for Gloria to do so as well. Emilio agreed to the terms.

Looking back on this pivotal career moment in her life, Gloria says, "I . . . joined . . . because I loved music, not because I wanted to perform. I didn't want to be in the spotlight, didn't desire it. . . . It never crossed my mind that this is what I'd do the rest of my life. I wanted to be a psychologist."

Because there were now two female members of the band, the group changed its name to the Miami Sound Machine (MSM). One of the first engagements the newly titled group performed was at the Dupont Plaza Hotel in Miami Beach, in the fall of 1975. There Gloria sang "What a Difference a Day Makes."

Avoiding the Spotlight

At the time Gloria joined Miami Sound Machine she was still exceedingly shy. It was a great obstacle to her performing effectively. She explained, "When I was singing, I always stared at the floor. Performing wasn't enjoyable for me. What I loved most about the band when I joined was the rehearsals, putting the music together. . . . The performance part was something I did because I had to. And I was so secure being behind the guys."

Before long, however, things changed and no longer were she and Merci just providing backup vocals and playing the maracas. Gloria says, "When they started pushing me out in front, it was hard. It was kind of baptism by fire there. The first time I had to sing apart from the band, it was just me and the soloist, and the rest of the band was about fifty feet behind me. I was like 'Aargh! My umbilical cord.' But it makes you grow, you know."

To help Gloria overcome her serious stage fright, Emilio told her that when she was front and center on stage to imagine that she was just performing for relatives and friends at home. He suggested she should act the same way in front of the band's audiences as she did in her own living room. Recalling this difficult apprenticeship period, Gloria says, "Just growing into the sheer enjoyment of what I do has taken time. I just try to do more of what I did in the living room of my house. And that's the whole idea, approaching it in that way." She soon began adding undemanding dance routines to her performances. In this transition period it was a constant battle to overcome her deep-seated bashfulness. However, she was determined to overcome her inhibitions and constantly to expand her performance techniques.

As part of the band, Gloria sang all types of music as the Miami Sound Machine geared their selections to match the tastes of each audience. Older crowds favored middle-of-the-road pop standards. The younger set liked rock numbers. Sometimes the songs were sung in Spanish, other times in English. Naturally, when they performed at events in the Cuban community, the song lineup featured numbers from their island homeland, including catchy conga numbers geared to make listeners stand up and dance. As one member of Miami Sound Machine said, "Our sound evolved from trying to please all the people. Here in Miami, we have Cubans, Anglos, blacks, South Americans. You have to be very versatile."

In gaining confidence to perform for onlookers, Gloria became aware that some members of the audience—usually more conservative, older people of the Cuban district—were unhappy to see a woman singing salsa music, numbers traditionally performed by men. (Salsa is Latin American music blending Cuban rhythms with ingredients of jazz, rock, and soul.) However, because her upbringing taught her to avoid limiting herself because of social restraints placed on women, Gloria did her best to ignore any such sexist complaints.

Gloria gained strength in her convictions about equality for women from examples in her own family. She explains, "I came from very strong women role models, my mother and my grandmother. My mother always taught you can do anything you want, and there was never any talk of well, you are a woman and you can't do this. Gloria's grandmother also encouraged her to pursue a singing career. She told her granddaughter, "This is your talent in life. This is what you do. It's a sin and crime if you don't go with what you do."

Another great inspiration for Gloria (since childhood) was Cuban-born Celia Cruz (1924–2003), one of Latin music's most revered vocalists. One of 14 children born in a small village outside of Havana, Celia was drawn to singing at an early age. It was not long before she began entering and winning local talent shows. Later she began singing professionally. In 1950 she joined the band La Sonora Matancero and soon began her recording career. In 1962 Cruz married Pedro Knight, the band's trumpet player.

Latin singer Celia Cruz, known as the Queen of Salsa, was a great influence on Gloria's career. (Landov)

Over the years Celia (known as the Queen of Salsa) and her musicians toured the world, pleasing audiences with their appealing Afro-Cuban rhythms. Meanwhile, when Fidel Castro's government tightened its control over Cuba in the early 1960s, Cruz and her husband refused to return to their homeland. Instead, they went to Mexico. Thereafter they settled in the U.S. and, eventually, became American citizens. In 1966, Celia joined Tito

Puente's orchestra. Later she performed with, among others, trombonist Johnny Pacheco who was a co-owner of the Fania (the sister music label to Vaya for whom she recorded for years). Late in her career the celebrated diva gained additional recognition when she appeared in such Hollywood feature films as *The Mambo Kings* (1992) and *The Perez Family* (1995). Always singing in Spanish, Celia Cruz continued to record right up to the end of her life in 2003 when she died of a brain tumor. (On Gloria's 2000 album, *Alma Caribeña,* Cruz made a guest appearance on one number.)

Gaining Self-Confidence

From the start of their association Gloria had romantic feelings for Emilio. However, she had no dating experience and knew that he socialized frequently, often with older women. She thought she had no chance with him. Emilio had been drawn immediately to Gloria. As he quickly learned of her difficult childhood and her ongoing sadness due to her very sick father, Estefan decided that he would not even consider dating her until he was sure of his feelings. He told his mother, "I am not going to make a move on this girl unless I am serious. She's been through too much." His greatest fear was to start a romantic relationship with her that might spoil their professional working relationship or harm their growing friendship.

Thus, for nearly a year, Emilio kept his true emotions from Gloria.

On July 4, 1976, about a year after they began to become acquainted, Miami Sound Machine was playing at a party celebrating America's bicentennial. The gig was aboard a ship in Miami. During one of the band's breaks, Emilio and Gloria went on deck to gaze at the stars. Joking that it was his birthday and that he wanted a kiss from her as a present, Gloria gave him an affectionate kiss. This prompted Emilio to tell Gloria how much he cared for her, and the two began dating.

Now sparked by having a most desirable man who adored her, Gloria decided to add dieting and exercise to her busy schedule which already included college classes, her part-time job as a translator, and rehearsing and performing with Miami Sound Machine.

Always anxious to motivate and inspire Gloria, one day Emilio told her that she still needed to improve herself by 95 percent. At first she found the remark insulting. She snapped, "If you think I could improve myself ninety-five percent, then why are you bothering with me now? You only like five percent of me? What if I don't improve? What if I don't change?" When she calmed down, she soon realized the wisdom of his latest challenge. According to her, "Emilio saw a side of me that I didn't let people see. He was trying to make me confident. . . . People mistook

In her early days as a performer, Gloria was forced to overcome her shyness. (WireImage)

my shyness for being stuck up. A performer can't afford to be shy."

Pushed by her caring boyfriend and buoyed by her growing sense of self-worth, Gloria began to remold her body and to dress more flatteringly to match her emerging good looks.

In 1978 Gloria, having majored in psychology and communications, graduated with a B.A. degree from the University of Miami. Rather than pursue a career as a psychologist she joined Miami Sound Machine on a full-time basis. Despite not directly using her particular college training as the basis of a career, Gloria was glad that she had gained a college education and she found ways to use her specialized knowledge in other ways. For example, she says, "I constantly auto-analyze myself."

In February 1978, she and Emilio became engaged to be married. On Saturday, September 2, 1978, the day after Gloria's 21st birthday, the couple were wed in a small ceremony in Miami. Because her ailing father was still confined to the hospital, he could not attend the wedding. Rather than have a substitute accompany her down the aisle, she walked alone. Right after the ceremony, Gloria, still in her wedding dress, and Emilio drove to the hospital to pay their respects to Mr. Fajardo. She was apprehensive that, as in recent years, he would not recognize her or understand that she had just been married. However, when the couple got to the sick man's bedside and she explained she was a new bride, her dad smiled at her and said, "Glorita." (It was his nickname for little Gloria, who shared her first name with her mother.)

Buoyed by this touching hospital visit, the newlyweds flew to Japan on their honeymoon.

4

STRUGGLING FOR SUCCESS

In 1979, months after Gloria wed Emilio Estefan, his older brother, José, decided it was time for he and his family to leave Cuba. However, Fidel Castro's regime had made it increasingly difficult for citizens to depart the country. Somehow José's plans became known to local officials. He and his family were forced to go into hiding for several weeks until they could work out their departure.

During this difficult time for José, Gloria and Emilio traveled to Cuba—their first trip there since each had left the country years before. Once on the island they found ways to sneak food and money to José and his family. Eventually, through contacts that the Estefans had with individuals in the Costa Rican government, they were able to arrange a visa for José and his kin.

In the midst of this errand of mercy Gloria had an opportunity to see the conditions of her former homeland in person. She was dismayed by what she saw: an impoverished country under the control of a communist dictatorship where the average individual counted for little. Gloria promised herself that she would never return to Cuba as long as Castro remained in power.

A Band with a Name

With ambitious, shrewd Emilio Estefan managing the band (as well as playing percussion), Miami Sound Machine continued to rise in popularity. In 1977, on a tiny budget of $2,000, they recorded their first album, *Renacer,* for the independent Audio Latino label in Miami. (The album would later be reissued under its English translation title, *Live Again.*) Because Emilio wanted his group to reach a broader audience, he insisted some of the songs be recorded in Spanish, and others in English. The debut disc—especially the title cut, "Renacer"—was sufficiently popular that the group made two additional independently released albums (1978's *Miami Sound Machine* and 1979's *Imported.*)

As Miami Sound Machine became more popular, they began composing original material. Their fusion of pop, disco, and salsa soon earned them a devoted following. Drawing on her love of poetry and her childhood experience of writing songs, Gloria soon began contributing numbers for the group's repertoire, particularly ballads.

By now Emilio realized that, in order for his band to really succeed, they needed the backing of a major record label. But finding a label is no simple feat in the highly competitive music industry. Enterprising Estefan used his marketing experience to promote Miami Sound Machine. All the disc jockeys in the Miami nightclubs were given free copies of the group's latest albums and singles, and local radio stations were aware of the group's newest tracks. Thanks to Emilio's promotional skills—and the band's talents—Miami Sound Machine quickly became the city's most popular dance band.

In 1980 Emilio decided that if his organization was to make the next step upward professionally, he must be available to guide the band full time. Thus, he quit Bacardi Imports after 12 years of service. Now able to devote himself fully to promoting his group's talents, he went into high gear with marketing and networking efforts. Within a relatively short time, the group was signed to a recording contract by Discos CBS International, the Miami-based branch of the powerful CBS Records label. Their first release was 1980's *MSM*. At the request of the label, all the tracks were recorded in Spanish and aimed at the company's global Latin market.

Also in 1980 two other major events occurred for the Estefans. On September 2, two years to the day of her marriage to Emilio, Gloria gave birth to their first child, Nayib. Countering the joy of the new addition to the family was the death—in this same period—of José Manuel Fajardo. It was the finale to her father's 12 long years of suffering.

Being Her Own Critic

Now that Gloria was a full-time professional musician in a fast-rising band, she was determined to improve her presentation on stage. She says, "I felt I had something in me I wanted to bring out. I just didn't know how to do it. It was a painful process, but I forced myself to do it, mostly by watching myself on videotape, which is the most horrendous experience there is. But it's the only way you can see what other people are seeing."

In this ongoing process of professional self-improvement, Gloria began to incorporate more intricate dance moves into her performance, blending her natural enthusiasm and sincerity with her drive to *really* entertain the audience through vocals and visuals. Audiences were quick to respond to the increasingly vivacious and energetic singer. The positive results encouraged Gloria to always seek new ways to improve her performance—a process that continues right up to the present day. (She told one interviewer, "I'm a perfectionist and once I was [in the spotlight] it was do it right or get out.")

Despite being a new mother, Gloria refused to slow her expanding career. Caught between being a traditional full-time parent and a working mother, she chose

the latter. She reasoned, "I don't feel that you're sup-
posed to give up your career for your children." She
explained further, "When you give up something of
yourself, you're usually not as happy as you were
before. And if you're not happy with yourself, it's very
hard to make someone else happy." Thus little Nayib
was brought along to his parents' rehearsals, sound studio sessions, and sometimes their performances. When
it proved impractical to have the youngster with them,
he was cared for by Gloria's mother or sister or by one
of Emilio's family.

Although Emilio felt it was limiting their potential
growth, their record label insisted that MSM's next albums
(including 1981's *Otra Vez* [Another Time], 1982's *Rio*
[River], and 1984's *A Toda Máquina* [At Full Speed]) also be
recorded in Spanish for distribution to the international
marketplace. As a result, their latest discs were promoted
only in Latin markets, and often contained the group's
catchy Spanish versions of American pop numbers. The
record company sent them on tours in Central and South
America where they performed in front of large crowds
(often over 40,000 people) in huge soccer stadiums.
Increasingly, Gloria took center stage. Accepting the challenge of entertaining such massive audiences, she repeatedly won the crowds' admiration for her growing performance skills.

Over these years of non-stop work MSM experienced top hits in such countries as Honduras, Panama, Peru, and Venezuela. Explaining their success Gloria told *New York Newsday*, "The reason we were able to cross over in all the countries in Latin America was that we had a pop sound. Each one of these countries has their own folkloric sound. We were able to cross, because to them we're a North American group that sang in Spanish, but it was very much pop music."

Reaching for Greater Fame

In 1982, there were several changes in Miami Sound Machine. Feeling that Emilio Estefan was receiving too much of the credit for the group's mounting success, Raul Murciano, one of the original members, left the band. When he departed, so did Gloria's cousin, Merci Navarro, who was now married to Raul. Because guiding, managing, and promoting Miami Sound Machine was increasingly a full-time task, Emilio cut back his performing in concerts with the group (although he continued for a time to participate in recording sessions). Because of the wealth of talent in the Miami marketplace, the Estefans were soon able to fill all the available openings.

By 1984 the contract between Discos CBS International and MSM terminated. Rather that stay with the Hispanic division of CBS Records, the group signed a pact with Epic, another CBS label that specialized in rock music for the international market.

Initially Epic executives were convinced that Miami Sound Machine's future lay in continuing to record songs in Spanish. Emilio insisted that English-language audiences were ripe for the group's special dance sound and that they needed to cater to this big marketplace. Epic remained firm, and the group prepared to record the "B" side of their upcoming new single in Spanish. (The "B" side is the flip side of a single-record release, one which the label feels will get far less air time or buyer interest than the song offered on the "A" side.) The tune in question was "Dr. Beat," composed by the band's Enrique "Kiki" Garcia who initially provided the lyrics in English. As had become customary, Gloria was to translate the words into Spanish for the recording session. However, she had difficulty in finding the right flow in her translation. Taking her problem to Emilio he, in turn, decided this might be fate telling them that the number should be sung in English. He met with Epic executives who, once again, insisted that the number be recorded in Spanish.

Not giving up, the band's founder argued that performers such as Spain's Julio Iglesias were experiencing crossover success (i.e., gaining popularity in more than one music format) by singing numbers in English that were played on bilingual stations with Latin formats and other outlets with an American pop format. Although Epic still remained unconvinced of Estefan's argument, they finally relented under Emilio's constant pressure. The song was recorded with its English lyrics.

When "Dr. Beat" was issued, the Latin-flavored disco number was soon being played both on stations featuring a Latin format and those that specialized in American pop. With its strong percussive beat, "Dr. Beat" was especially appropriate for airing at disco clubs then the rage in the U.S. It was in these popular nightclubs that the song gained a strong following. (The song would soon rise to

Miami Sound Machine band members: (from left) Emilio Estefan, Marcos Avila, Gloria Estefan, and Kiki Garcia (Photofest)

number 10 position on *Billboard* magazine's dance chart.) "Dr. Beat" was launched overseas and became a success.

Launching the Crossover Album

Pleased by the success of "Dr. Beat," Epic agreed to Miami Sound Machine releasing a full English-language album. Entitled *Eyes of Innocence,* the 1984 album contained "Dr. Beat" plus four other entries by Kiki Garcia. Gloria contributed two numbers ("Love Me" and "When Someone Comes into Your Life"). Other band members provided the album's three other cuts. Disappointingly, the album did not take off in the United States. However, the group remained positive. They embarked on a concert tour in the Netherlands and England.

While playing in Amsterdam, Gloria had the notion that their stage show should include a flavorful conga. Initially, Emilio didn't favor the idea but soon agreed to go along with his wife's concept. At MSM's next concert they ended their performance with a conga number sung in Spanish. The audience was wildly enthusiastic. Inspired by the crowd's reaction Gloria suggested that Kiki Garcia create a new song—one with a strong conga beat and lyrics in English. He complied with a number he called simply "Conga."

Back in the U.S., Epic management was not excited by Miami Sound Machine's new specialty number. One executive remarked that the song was "too Latin for the

Americas and too American for the Latins." Rather than be annoyed by this response, Gloria was pleased. She explained to the man that his statement exactly fit their band, which could make a real crossover success with this song. Reacting to Gloria's great confidence and enthusiasm, the record company finally allowed "Conga" to be produced as an English-language release.

To everyone's amazement—except the members of Miami Sound Machine—"Conga" was a hit on both sides of the Atlantic Ocean. By September 1985 the cut was on *Billboard*'s dance chart and by the next February had reached number 10 position. To everyone's astonishment—including the band—the song landed on four different *Billboard* charts: dance, pop, Latin, and African American. This was the first time in the history of the American music industry that such an achievement had been accomplished. As a result of this breakthrough song, Gloria Estefan and Miami Sound Machine became instantly recognizable names to contemporary music lovers everywhere.

Miami Sound Machine was soon back in the recording studio making a new album, *Primitive Love* (1985). Besides including the sensational "Conga," the disc contained several numbers written by three new additional members to the band, who brought their special sound to the group. The trio was Lawrence Dermer, Joe Galdo, and Rafael

Vigil, who billed themselves as The Three Jerks. They provided several highlight numbers for Gloria to sing, including the title tune and the disco entry, "Bad Boy." Gloria composed one of the disc's 10 cuts. Entitled "Words Get in the Way," her romantic dance song came about after having quarreled with Emilio and deciding she had not put across her best points in their heated discussion. Left alone she plucked at her guitar and came up with this winning number.

For Gloria, songwriting was a serious and artistically challenging matter. "Writing," she explained, "is the most difficult thing for me. It's a process. Like having a baby. It starts and it finishes. And each song is so unique and so separate. It's hard to know where I'm ever going to get the next one. But somehow it comes—through life. You keep living and you have experiences, and this or that will inspire you. Hopefully, it will keep coming." (Typically Gloria and her colleagues would not merely translate the lyrics from one language to another. Instead they composed individual sets of lyrics—one in English, one in Spanish—for versions of the songs in each language. Their extra effort insured that the lyrics in each language properly fit the melody.)

When *Primitive Love* was released, it featured a portrait of Gloria alone on the cover, proving how central she had become to the group's public image. (On the back side were pictures of Gloria, Emilio, Kiki Garcia, and Juan

Avila, but not the Three Jerks.) In addition to "Conga," "Words Get in the Way" and "Bad Boy" became sizeable hits. In worldwide release, *Primitive Love* sold over 4 million copies, making it a noteworthy commercial success.

In support of the new album, Miami Sound Machine embarked on an American concert tour. In person, percussionist Kiki Garcia continued to be an enthusiastic cutup, frequently sharing the limelight with Gloria. For Gloria's part, she proved increasingly to be a crowd-pleaser, mixing her vocals with uncomplicated dance steps as she moved joyfully about the stage. Audiences joined in, typically dancing in the aisles during their concerts.

On the tour, the band would wind up the evening's festivities by performing their famous "Conga." So infectious was this song's beat that when the group did it at a Vermont venue, some 11,000 concertgoers were reportedly inspired to form the world's longest conga line and happily danced (three steps forward followed by a kick) to the joyous Cuban music. (Later, in 1988, MSM created a new entry for the Guinness Book of Records when in their hometown at the local Calle Ocho Festival in the city's "Little Havana," they performed "Conga." In enthusiastic response the delighted audience formed a conga line that boasted 119,000 participants!)

By now there was no doubt that Miami Sound Machine was a major crossover success.

5

RISING TO THE TOP

The release of *Primitive Love*—and the band's subsequent
global tours—proved that Miami Sound Machine was a
very successful enterprise. As a result Emilio and Gloria
formed Estefan Enterprise Inc., a business organization
geared for handling their growing success and branching
out into other commercial ventures. That same year, 1986,
Gloria placed her footprints on the Boulevard of Stars in
Amsterdam—a celebrity walkway in the Netherlands similar to Hollywood's Walk of Fame (where Estefan would
later receive her own sidewalk star). At the 1986 Tokyo
Music Fair, Miami Sound Machine, representing the U.S.,
won first prize.

It was during this Tokyo engagement that Miami
Sound Machine realized how popular they had become
abroad. According to Gloria, "In Japan they had told us,
'Don't feel bad if you just hear polite applause because the

Japanese are very reserved people, that's how they are.' Then after the first song, they all jumped out of their seats and were dancing for the whole show. They came up on the stage at the end of the show and danced with us."

Back in Miami, the Estefans were already regarded as icons by the city's multicultural population. The couple was praised for their clean living, which included no drugs, no liquor, and not promoting sexuality in their songs. For Cubans, the Estefans and their music embodied a wonderful mix of their traditional culture fused with new American trends. The successful duo also symbolized the great American dream where anyone—no matter how humble their start in the U.S.—could achieve great artistic and commercial triumphs.

Capitalizing on Success

Despite the success of *Primitive Love*, there was concern at the Epic label that this accomplishment might have been a fluke and that Miami Sound Machine's achievement was no guarantee that its next album would duplicate its popularity with a broad base of record buyers. To insure the group's continued appeal, the record company refined the band's image. Because of Gloria's prominence, the group was renamed Gloria Estefan and Miami Sound Machine.

To more effectively market Gloria, the band's focal artist, Epic guided her through a program to further refine her professional image. This included redefining her hair style and makeup, and encouraging her to hire a personal trainer to tone up her shape and physical condition. Soon Gloria and her band made their debut in a new medium—music videos. For Estefan, being in front of the all-seeing camera was a nerve-wracking experience, but one she knew was necessary to promote the group on such cable TV networks as MTV and VH1. She survived the taping ordeal by telling herself that she must conquer this new medium.

For Miami Sound Machine's new album, 1987's *Let It Loose*, the Three Jerks contributed five songs (including the title tune and "I Want You So Bad"), Gloria and Kiki Garcia supplied three numbers (including "1-2-3"), and Estefan alone provided "Anything for You." This song represented Gloria the songwriter at her most efficient. She always carried notebooks with her to jot down ideas and possible lyrics for future songs. One day, just before a recording session, she sat in a coffee shop eating a hamburger. Within a few minutes there she jotted down the lyrics for "Anything for You," the last song on the album to be recorded. That accomplished, Gloria rushed over to the sound studio and ran through the number with the other musicians and it went well. Days later, after needed adjustments to the musical arrangement, the band recorded a final take of the cut. Everyone was pleased with the song except Epic executives. Emilio insisted to his label bosses that the song would be a major hit.

Emilio's forecast proved to be accurate. By May 14, 1988, "Anything for You" had risen to the top position on the *Billboard* pop chart. The ballad went on to be nominated for a Grammy in the category of Best Pop Vocal Performance by a Duo or Group With Vocal. (Other songs from this album also were hits, including "Rhythm Is Gonna Get You.") The album, which remained solidly on the music charts for over two years, drew critical praise for its "jazzy Latino flavor" (*Rolling Stone*). It went on to sell over 4 million copies worldwide. For their work on the new album, Gloria and Miami Sound Machine won an American Music Award that year.

With the band now fully in the mainstream and Gloria launched into superstar status (some music journalists now referred to her as "the Latina Madonna") there was increased interest in Estefan's talent as a songwriter and especially her choices of emotional moods for her lyrics. She told one interviewer, "The main thing people always ask me is, 'How come you write these (sad) ballads when supposedly you're happily married and you're very happy' . . . and I am. But I think that's where the artist uses his creative license. I might have experienced these feelings a while back or maybe vicariously through somebody else, maybe friends of mine that have gone through a similar thing. I think the artist always writes from within, from the soul, and even if you didn't experience it yourself, you have to feel how would people in this situation feel, and how would they say it. I always try to write very conversationally . . . and then I try to make it more musical."

In 1989, Gloria and Miami Sound Machine won an American Music Award for best duo or group. (Associated Press)

To further promote *Let It Loose,* Gloria and the band returned to the road. This time, because six-year-old Nayib Estefan was so involved with playing Little League baseball games in Miami, he stayed at home with Emilio. Also not on this tour were the Three Jerks, who had contributed so much to the songs on the new album. Now focusing on songwriting, arranging, and producing their numbers, they no longer performed on stage with Gloria. Other musicians were recruited to fill their spots.

Gloria and Miami Sound Machine played sold-out engagements across the United States and then in Canada, Spain, the Netherlands, England, Italy, and Japan. Wherever the group appeared, Gloria was in the key spotlight, delighting audiences with her rich, full-bodied voice and enticing stage moves. On this trek one of her most emotionally rewarding engagements was singing for U.S. soldiers stationed in the demilitarized zone between North and South Korea. (Film of this event was telecast in connection with the 1998 Summer Olympics held in Seoul, Korea.)

Although concertgoers everywhere around the globe enthusiastically welcomed the band, such was not the case in Cuba, where the group was banned from playing. Castro's government also ordered that their albums were not to be sold in stores, nor were their songs broadcast on the island's radio stations. It soon became popular practice among

Cuban there to sneak contraband Miami Sound Machine albums into the island country for secret listening at home.

Because of the sanctions against Gloria and her band in her homeland, there was some controversy when it was announced that Estefan and Miami Sound Machine would perform at the August 1987 Pan American Games held in Indianapolis. Cuba was among the 38 nations sending athletes to the sports competition. These athletes protested against Gloria and her group making an appearance at the celebration. Despite reported death threats, Gloria Estefan refused to yield to pressure and the band performed without incident.

The 20-month *Let It Loose* tour ended in Miami. The two final concerts at the city's arena were videotaped and edited for release as a Showtime cable TV special entitled *Homecoming Concert*. (The program won a trio of Cable ACE awards.) During her Miami performance Estefan dedicated her singing of "Words Get in the Way" to Julio Iglesias. The international music superstar, who was by now a good friend of the Estefans, was in the audience that evening.

With the global trek finished, Gloria settled down to spend time with Nayib and the rest of her family. Once so fearful of performing on stage, she now felt at a loss when not performing in front of a big audience. She explained, "When you get offstage with all these thousands of people loving you, the saddest part is to go back to your hotel room by yourself."

Changes

Marking the end of another stage in the evolution of Miami Sound Machine, Kiki Garcia departed the group, as did The Three Jerks. These personnel changes left Gloria as the last remaining original member of the group still performing with the band. She was now the chief focus of Miami Sound Machine and had great authority over how things should be handled on stage. Meanwhile, Emilio had become the guiding force behind the scene, handling business deals and making suggestions for new songs, new talent, and the group's creative direction. Thus, just as the couple's marriage was an equal partnership, so was their professional activity. This balance of control and duties was a relatively unique situation within the industry and both cherished this arrangement. As fresh musicians continued to join the organization, the Estefans made every effort to welcome them as part of their close-knit extended family. (Among the newcomers were keyboardist/songwriter Clay Ostwald, bassist/songwriter Jorge Casas, and guitarist/songwriter John DeFaria.)

On the home front, the now wealthy Estefans began remodeling an elaborate two-story, Spanish-style home on Star Island, located on Miami's Biscayne Bay. Over the next several years, the multi-million dollar estate would include two other structures: a spacious guesthouse, and, across the road, a comfortable home for Emilio's parents.

In 1988 Gloria joined with Peter Gabriel, Sting, and other musicians in the Amnesty International "Human Rights Now!" concert tour. That summer she performed a duet with famous tenor Placido Domingo at a Central Park concert in New York City. The musical pairing was so successful that the duo later recorded "Hasta Amarte" for the opera singer's CBS album, *Goya . . . A Life in Song* (1989). For this track Estefan provided a Spanish-language adaptation of the song, "Till I Loved You."

For the July 1989 release, *Cuts Both Ways*, Gloria was now billed as a solo artist, and the name Miami Sound Machine no longer appeared on the album's cover. Emilio explained the reason for this change. "She's been the lead singer for years but no one knows her name. They always called her 'that girl from the Miami Sound Machine." For the Grammys, she could only be nominated in the group category, not as a singer. This was the record company's idea, and I like it."

The new album's title referred to the fact that some of the songs were sung in Spanish, others in English. Of the six numbers that Gloria wrote for the release, "Don't Wanna Lose You" was the first single to be issued. Written for her husband, the emotional ballad rose to number one on the *Billboard* pop charts that September. It was nominated for a Grammy in the category of Best Pop Vocal Performance, Female, but Gloria lost the prize. Another of the tracks on the highly successful album full of Latin-flavored dance numbers was the hit single "Here We Are." This ballad, arranged by Gloria, rose to number six position on the *Billboard* charts.

Explaining her attraction to ballad-writing, Estefan said, "Ballads are basically what I'm about. I just feel you can express yourself more completely and eloquently in a ballad. It's easier to identify with someone else and form a closer bond with the audience." (By now Gloria had learned to play the piano, which made her songwriting chores easier.) For her writing contributions to *Cuts Both Ways*, BMI—the performing rights organization representing songwriters, composers, and music publishers— recognized Estefan as 1989's Songwriter of the Year.

To publicize *Cuts Both Ways* Gloria and the band went on a European tour. Nayib, now nine, accompanied his parents on the trip, which was shorter than past ones. Returning to America, Gloria planned to give concerts around the U.S., including a gala at Madison Square Garden in New York City. However, while abroad she had contracted the flu and her fits of coughing had ruptured a blood vessel in her throat. As a result, her physician ordered her not to sing for at least two months.

In the Limelight

With her tremendous prominence within the music business, Gloria was made a presenter at both the 1990 American Music Awards and the Grammys. Two months later she received the Crystal Globe Award given to those performers whose albums have sold over 5 million copies abroad.

These impressive industry endorsements proved what the public had long known—that Estefan was a very special talent who, through songwriting, singing, and performing, made magical connections with her audiences. Meanwhile, her fan base was constantly increasing from her wide variety of media appearances. Besides her singles/albums being played on radio and jukeboxes, she was a frequent attraction on the concert stage and appeared in several music videos. Whether on albums, radio, music videos, or making TV guest appearances, Estefan seemed to be everywhere. This now included motion pictures. She and the Miami Sound Machine were among those in the 1986 TV movie *Club Med*. That same year, the band sang "Hot Summer Nights" on the soundtrack of the Tom Cruise theatrical release *Top Gun*. The next year the group's "Bad Boy" and "Conga" were utilized on the soundtrack of the big-screen comedy hit *Three Men and a Baby*, starring Tom Selleck and Ted Danson.

Once her throat condition healed, Gloria and her group returned to touring the U.S. Between engagements, on March 19, 1990, Gloria, Emilio, and Nayib visited the White House, where they met President George Bush and discussed her public service efforts to combat drug usage among America's youth. Leaving the White House, the Estefans felt that life could not be better. They had hit albums, were expanding their business

Gloria meets with President George H. W. Bush in 1990.
(Associated Press)

enterprises, were doing quite well financially, and they and their loved ones were all in good health.

The Estefans traveled to Manhattan to connect with their customized tour bus and head to their next concert engagement, scheduled for the evening of March 20 in Syracuse, New York. It was on this fateful trek that the Estefans' bus was involved in the disastrous road accident. That everyone aboard the vehicle survived the collision was a miracle. However, for Gloria, who was most seriously injured of those aboard, it was the start of a long, painful road to recovery.

6

COMING OUT
OF THE DARK

On that fateful March 1990 day near Scranton, Pennsylvania, where the tour bus had been rammed by a truck, badly injured Gloria lay on the vehicle's floor in excruciating pain. In recalling that torturous time, she says, "Believe me, I would rather give birth to ten kids in a row than go through that kind of pain again."

Later, when Gloria was flown to New York City to undergo an operation at the Orthopedic Institute Hospital for Joint Diseases, her distraught mother was there. Also present was celebrated salsa singer Celia Cruz, a good friend of the severely hurt celebrity. In the coming days, such was the outpouring of concern for Gloria from well-wishers around the globe—especially from Miami—that Estefan received an estimated 50,000 get-well messages and 4,000 flower arrangements. (In Miami, as a special tribute to one of their own, local radio stations played Gloria's recordings nonstop.)

After the successful four-hour surgery, which included repairing a pinched nerve that the singer had before the mishap, the patient remained hospitalized for nearly two weeks. (The doctors informed Emilio that had his wife's spine moved even another half-inch after the bus accident she would have been permanently paralyzed.) When it came time for Gloria to be discharged from the facility, the singer, ever aware of her responsibility to the caring public, insisted upon attending a press conference at the hospital. Arriving at the meeting in a wheelchair, she astounded the media by standing up! She informed the press that, within a few months, she was sure she would be in good health once again. Then, with family members, she traveled by limousine to the airport where she boarded Julio Iglesias's private jet for the flight to Florida. When the plane reached Miami International Airport, several hundred fans were there to provide the patient with moral support.

Clutching Emilio's arm as she coped with severe pain, Gloria insisted on walking out of the plane. She stopped to wave to the cheering crowd, telling them, "I want you to know that I've felt every one of your prayers from the first moment." To add a bit of humor to the highly emotional moment, she joked about the steel rods in her back: "I hope I don't ring [the alarms] all the time now when I go through those things (i.e., metal detectors) at the airport."

Hard Work and Prayers

Once back at her Star Island home in Miami, Gloria understood that she had an exceedingly difficult path ahead not only to regain her full mobility, but to be able also to exert the energy necessary for her stage performances. In the first days back in Florida she began brooding about her bad luck and how to cope with the lengthy recovery regimen that lay ahead. From her college studies of psychology she understood she was undergoing the normal stages of adjusting to the trauma and the anxiety of dealing with its after-effects. To counteract these negative feelings, she reminded herself, "You can't let life just land on you. Bad things happen of course, but you have to take control of your life."

She also admitted to herself (and to others) in this post-accident period, "I'm more relaxed now. I was always thinking that things were going too well. Something was going to happen. And now it has. I figure I'm good now for another few years. When I think of what could have happened, I feel better—and luckier—every day."

Part of Gloria's immediate therapy required that, at least once every 45 minutes, she get out of bed—no matter how painful it was—and take a short walk. Emilio was on round-the-clock duty to escort his spouse on these agonizing exercise steps geared to prevent her muscles from going rigid. Recalling this grueling procedure, Emilio said, "She used to walk and cry at the same time."

What especially helped Gloria's recovery was the fact that she was in such good physical condition beforehand and that she was an extremely disciplined, self-motivated individual. As part of her recuperation procedure she undertook water therapy by swimming three times a week. She also began a schedule of extensive daily exercise under the guidance of a personal trainer. Each day saw a small degree of improvement. As the weeks passed, she celebrated each tiny victory, which—given the circumstances—were big achievements (e.g., washing her face, putting on her shoes, dressing herself).

Back in the Winner's Circle

During the months of exhausting, painful therapy, Gloria focused on her strong desire to return as soon as humanly possible to her show business career. Her drive to recover motivated this highly determined woman to push her endurance level to make her recovery more complete as soon as possible.

For the annual Labor Day Jerry Lewis Telethon in 1990, the singer provided a video message in which she urged the public to donate to this charity drive, which combats muscular dystrophy, a crippling illness similar to the one that killed her father. She also used the occasion to tell her many fans that she was well on the road to recovery and planned to be back performing soon.

In actuality, Gloria was already back to songwriting. She described, "I was apprehensive about getting back into writing, and I didn't know what would come out of it or if anything would. My husband had been in one of the helicopters [after the crash] traveling from one hospital to the other. It was really dark and gray, and he was traumatized. He got this ray of light that hit him in the face, and he got the idea for 'Coming Out of the Dark.' About three months later he came to me and said, 'When you start writing again, I have a song I want to co-write with you.' [Later] when I came in, he was putting the melody to it, and when I sat there, it all poured out."

It was in June of 1990 that Gloria first felt herself truly on the road to recovery and that she was, indeed, coming out of the dark. "It took that long for me to be unaided—to walk, go to the bathroom, get dressed. Up until that point, it was up in the air when I would recover, because there had been lots of nerve damage." In this extended mending period one of her biggest emotional obstacles was to overcome her nervousness at riding in a car. In her typical fashion, Estefan combated this fear and moved on to fresh challenges. On the positive side she pointed out, "It's very hard to stress me out now. It's hard to get me in an uproar about anything because most things have little significance compared with what I almost lost." She also observed jokingly, "I would not recommend a brush with death to anybody, but if you are going to have it, at least get some good stuff out of it."

As Gloria prepared material for the new album (1991's *Into the Light*), she made sure that the new release would not dissolve into what she termed "the accident album." She explained to the Los Angeles *Daily News*, "I hate pity. I'm very self-reliant and independent, and I'm used to that role. I don't like people feeling sorry for me. So I wrote 'Coming Out of the Dark' to let the people around me know how important they are to me. But that was as far as I wanted to go with the accident." To bolster her spirits, and the mood of the new album, she channeled all the positive energy about her. "I used everybody's prayers—I could feel that energy focused on me. . . . Most performers have to die to elicit such an outpouring of love. I was lucky to feel that, and it will touch me for the rest of my life." In shaping *Into the Light*, Gloria noted, "I wanted this album to be a very freeing experience for me. I wanted my vocal performances to be much more emotional. . . . I was very happy when I started singing again, and I wanted to share that feeling."

The new album's big hit was her victory number, "Coming Out of the Dark." It was created by the Estefans and Jon Secada, a relatively new member of the band. In fact, the Cuban-born Secada contributed to the composition of several of the disc's 13 tracks as well as providing background vocals and music arrangement. "Coming Out of the Dark" would go to the top of the *Billboard* music charts in March 1991. Other entries conceived by Gloria included "Nayib's Song," a tribute to her love for her son, and "Sex in the '90s," about the dangers of casual sex in today's world.

As the new album was being launched, Estefan returned to the concert stage. On March 1 she opened her *Into the Light* world tour in Miami. She enthused, "There was no way I could have started anywhere else. I've just felt so much support and love that Miami had to be the first show. They'll also be forgiving—if I get choked up, they'll probably get choked up, too."

While the latest album proved very successful and showed Estefan had regained all her skills, several contemporary music critics noted that Gloria now was directing her attention more to the middle-of-the-road audience than to the young crowd. As a result her new music found its greatest success in the adult contemporary marketplace.

Launching Ahead

By early 1992 Estefan was back in the U.S. from her world tour. During the halftime show at that year's Super Bowl in Minneapolis, she sang exuberant renditions of "Get on Your Feet" and "Live for Loving You." That May she received a lifetime achievement honor from Premio Lo Nuestro a la Musica Latina, the Latin American equivalent to the Grammys.

As part of their mushrooming business enterprises, the Estefans had already established the Crescent Moon Studios, a state-of-the-art recording facility on Bird Road in Miami. Now they purchased the art deco-style Cardoza Hotel in Miami's trendy South Beach district. One of their first innovations there was to open Larios on the Beach, a Cuban-American restaurant that quickly gained a distinctive reputation for its fine cuisine and chic atmosphere. Later, among other corporate expansions, the Estefans would debut an impressive, huge dining establishment, Bongo's Cuban Café, at Disney World in Orlando, Florida.

Believing strongly in giving back to the community, Gloria and Emilio responded to the havoc created by Hurricane Andrew that hit southern Florida in August 1992. Later, they visited some of the devastated parts of the state. This prompted their helping to organize a benefit concert on behalf of victims of Hurricane Andrew. Held at Joe Robbie Stadium in Miami, over 53,000 individuals attended the September 26, 1992 fund-raiser. The charitable event raised over $4 million. Estefan wrote a special song ("Always Tomorrow") that became closely associated with the storm relief campaign.

As part of Gloria's public service work (which would later include starting a foundation to assist a variety of causes), she agreed to spend three months in 1993 as a special delegate to the United Nations, serving on the

Third Committee on Human Rights. During her tenure she had the opportunity to make a public address at the UN regarding their hearings on conditions in Cuba.

In October 1992 Epic Records released Gloria's *Greatest Hits* album. The 14-song disc was well received, and it included numbers both with and without Miami Sound Machine. The next June came *Mi Tierra* [My Homeland], which featured all Spanish-language love songs. This entry, which paid tribute to her ethnic roots, went to number one on the Latin pop chart, while peaking at number 27 on the *Billboard* 200 (album) chart. For this new work, Gloria contributed, among others, the title tune and "Mi Buen Amore" (My True Love) while the Estefans cowrote such numbers as "Tus Ojos" (Your Eyes). The critically well-regarded album won a Grammy trophy as Best Tropical album.

The spring of 1993 saw Gloria receive a great honor from the United States. In May she traveled to Ellis Island. Located in New York City's harbor, this was where many immigrants to America used to be processed before being admitted to the country. There Estefan received the Ellis Island Congressional Medal of Honor, the highest distinction the U.S. bestows on an individual born outside of America. Among her other awards during this period was an honorary doctorate from her alma mater, the University of Miami, and the Hispanic Heritage Award.

The New Child

Having survived her accident and having returned to a full and rewarding professional life, Gloria told Emilio that she wanted to have another child. This became the most important goal in her life. As such, she declined the offer to audition for the pending screen musical version of *Evita,* which was eventually made for 1996 release with Madonna. When Gloria could not conceive, physicians discovered that she had a crushed fallopian tube as a result of the bus accident. After undergoing surgery, Gloria soon was able to become pregnant. While awaiting the birth of her child, the singer recorded a new album, 1994's *Hold Me, Thrill Me, Kiss Me.* The disc's theme was to present 12 tunes that she had adored listening to on the radio as a young person and which had inspired her own songwriting and performing. Among the cuts were cover versions of Neil Sedaka's "Breaking Up Is Hard to Do" and Carole King's "It's Too Late." She made a music video for one of the album's tracks, "Turn the Beat Around". Another of the album's videos, "Everlasting Love," spotlighted Gloria Estefan impersonators dressed in her old costumes.

On December 5, 1994, Gloria gave birth to Emily Marie Estefan. Family friend Quincy Jones, the musician and entrepreneur, agreed to be the baby's godfather. A week after the delivery, the Estefans—including Nayib and Emily—made an appearance on Oprah Winfrey's TV talk show.

Emilio, Gloria, and their daughter, Emily (WireImage)

Taking a break from concert performing to spend time with her family, Gloria turned out two albums in 1995. The first, released in September, was *Abriendo Puertas* [Opening Doors]. Her second Spanish-language album released in the U.S., the disc featured songs that highlighted Latin American culture and utilized Latin music from countries around the world. The disc, which contained many Christmas and New Year numbers, earned Gloria her second Grammy, this time in the category of Best Tropical Latin Performance. (At the Grammy ceremonies that year, Estefan sang "Abriendo Puertas," making her the first performer to perform a song in Spanish at this event.) The same month, Epic distributed Gloria's *Christmas Through Your Eyes*, filled with contemporary adult arrangements of holiday favorites, along with a new number (the title tune).

Also in September 1995, Gloria and Emilio again went to Cuba, their first time since 1979 when the couple had helped his brother and his family leave the country. Although she had sworn never to return to her homeland until Castro was no longer in power, she bent her rule. She flew to Guantánamo Bay, where the U.S. government has a naval base and where Cuban refugees had a safe refuge until they could be permitted to relocate to the United States. After touring the military installation Gloria performed songs for the audience composed of military personnel and refugees.

Dealing Again with Tragedy

Usually preoccupied with work, the Estefans rarely took a day just to relax. However, on September 24, 1995, they went out on their 30-foot boat. As usual, Biscayne Bay was packed with private boats, tourist vessels, and especially wet bikes. The latter are two-seat water crafts that ride like fast motorcycles as they skim over the waves. At the time there was no requirement for wet bike drivers to be licensed or even trained in using the speedy vehicles. As a result, there were frequent serious accidents involving their use.

On this day, a 29-year-old law student had rented a wet bike, which he shared with his girlfriend. Around 4 P.M. as Gloria and Emilio were returning to their private dock outside their home, the wet biker drove dangerously near their bigger craft, evidently trying to "jump a wake" (i.e. maneuvering through the churning water behind a larger motor boat in order to propel the wet bike into an airborne leap across the waves).

In the collision that resulted when the wet bike slammed into the side of the Estefans' pleasure boat, the young woman tumbled clear of the accident. However, the driver was pulled under the Estefans' craft and was badly sliced by the blades of the motor boat's twin propellers. Horrified by the situation, Emilio jumped into the water, intent on rescuing the injured man (from drowning or being attacked by sharks). Meanwhile Gloria called for 911 assistance. With the help of others nearby, the badly injured student was placed in the Estefans' craft and they raced to shore to meet the ambulance. Sadly, the victim died on the way to the hospital.

Shocked by this mishap, for which they were in no way guilty of wrongdoing, Gloria felt it was her responsibility to talk with the dead man's mother. She said making that call was, "harder than the bus accident." As more days passed, the singer became convinced that accidents such as this must finally be stopped. The next February she appeared at a hearing before the Florida House Committee on Natural Resources to voice her opinion on how to remedy the dangerous situation. Following her plea that wet bikers be made aware of how to operate these crafts and to be alerted to potential dangers, the state's Senate and House adopted into law a version of Estefan's proposal.

In the midst of this new crusade, Estefan accepted a request from Pope John Paul II to join in a celebration at the Vatican in Rome to honor the pontiff's 50th year as a priest. At the distinguished gathering, she sang "Más Allá" (Beyond) from her *Abriendo Puertas* album. Renewed by this experience, she returned home to Florida and began work on her next release.

7

THE INSPIRATIONAL DIVA

For Gloria Estefan's June 1996 album, *Destiny*, the singing star collaborated with Diane Warren on writing both the title tune and "I Know You Too Well." "Destiny," prepared for the 1996 Olympics held in Atlanta, Georgia, became the games' anthem and was performed by Estefan at the closing ceremonies of the sports competition. One of the disc's other numbers, "Along Came You (A Song for Emily)," written by Gloria, contained a few spontaneous words uttered by little Emily Estefan at a rehearsal taping for the song that were incorporated into the final release track.

Reflecting on the growing strength of her lyric-writing, Estefan observed, "I've lived through a lot of things in the past few years. Everything that you live and every emotional layer comes into your writing and your singing." To support her new disc, a blending of Latin and Cuban beats presented in an adult contemporary pop style, Gloria set out on a world tour—her first since before daughter Emily's birth in December 1994. This time the Estefans' 15-year-old son, Nayib, had a featured part in the elaborate show, performing magic tricks as the opening act.

A Much In-Demand Star

When Fidel Castro's communist government suddenly invited Pope John Paul II to visit Cuba in January 1998, the pontiff, in turn, asked Gloria to perform for him there. She politely declined the request. Estefan explained her decision to the *Miami Herald*. "My going there would have turned a beautiful spiritual thing into a political thing because I thought it was fantastic that the pope was going . . . . But me going there would have been very political. . . . I would have asked for permission from the Cuban government, which I'm not

In 1996 Gloria embarked on a World Tour to promote her album Destiny. *(Photofest)*

about to do, and it just would have been a slap in the face of my [late] father and everything he fought for."

In April 1998 Gloria joined with Mariah Carey, Céline Dion, Aretha Franklin, and Shania Twain for the VH1 cable network's first *Divas Live* concert, a fund-raiser to support music programs in schools. On this TV special Estefan had the opportunity to perform oncamera with her long-time idol, Carole King, in a rendition of "You've Got a Friend." Two months later, Estefan's album, *gloria!* was in stores. (There were two versions of the release, one for the U.S. and another for the global marketplace, which contained an add-on disco medley.)

In assessing *gloria!* for allmusic.com, Stephen Thomas Erlewine reported, "With its percolating disco beats and sunny melodies, the record recalls her glory days of the late '80s, but there is a stronger Latin rhythmic under-pinning which gives the music depth." The adventurous album went to number 23 on the *Billboard* 200 (album) chart, while the song "Heaven's What I Feel" rose to number 13 on the American pop rankings. Ironically, whereas in past years the Estefans had to battle repeatedly to release their music with English-language lyrics, now they had to push Epic Records to release "Oye" (Listen) as a single, because its lyrics were in Spanish.

Because Gloria had cut down on her concert tour schedule, she devoted more energy to making TV appearances to keep herself visible to her fans. In October 1998 she was showcased on A&E cable network. On the two-hour *Live by Request* she performed numbers requested by members of the studio audience as well as those calling in or sending e-mails. In January 1999 Estefan was the guest host on Rosie O'Donnell's TV talk show. At the end of that month, Gloria was the featured attraction at the halftime show at the Super Bowl, which was held at Pro Player Stadium in Miami. Besides performing solo numbers (including "Turn the Beat Around") she joined Stevie Wonder for a duet medley.

Tackling the Movies

Eager to expand her creative experiences to other aspects of show business, Gloria had long wanted to appear in a feature film. Earlier in the 1990s she had not pursued the opportunity to star in the movie musical, *Evita*. (She had also bypassed an offer to play the Latina lawyer in Michael Douglas's *Disclosure* [1994] because she was pregnant with her second child at the time.) Now, in searching for a screen assignment, she decided it would make sense to take a smaller part rather than tackle a lead role. (Gloria says, "I'm the type of person that needs time and wants to do things slowly.")

Thus Gloria was pleased to play Isabel Vasquez in *Music of the Heart* (1999). Based on a true-life account, the feel-good movie focuses on a young teacher (played by Meryl Streep) in Harlem who battles the Board of Education to continue her program of teaching underprivileged students the beauty of music through the violin. Besides her oncamera performance in the film, Gloria was also heard on the soundtrack singing the title song with the group NSync. At the Blockbuster Entertainment Awards, Gloria and NSync won in the Favorite Song From a Movie category. Estefan was also nominated for an ALMA trophy but lost in the Outstanding Actress category to Cameron Diaz (for *Any Given Sunday*).

Gloria and Meryl Streep in the film Music of the Heart. (Photofest)

Gloria next appeared on screen in *For Love of Country: The Arturo Sandoval Story,* which premiered on HBO cable on November 18, 2000. In this effective biographical drama, Havana-born Andy Garcia was cast in the title role of the famed Cuban trumpet player who, in the 1990s, received political asylum in the U.S. Others in the production included Charles S. Dutton as jazz great Dizzy Gillespie and Mia Maestrao as Sandoval's loving wife. (Gloria, who played the heroine's friend, was well acquainted with Sandoval. The veteran musician had been guest trumpeter on such Estefan albums as *Into the Light* and *Mi Tierra.*)

Estefan also received an Award of Merit at the 2000 American Music Awards celebrating her "outstanding contributions to the musical entertainment of the American public." That same year Gloria released *Alma Caribeña* (Caribbean Soul), her third Spanish-language album for the mainstream marketplace. Accenting the range of Latin flavors represented on the disc, Estefan sang one song each with Latin music icons Celia Cruz and José Feliciano. (Gloria won both a Grammy and a trophy at the 8th Billboard Latin Music Awards for this album. The music video to the song "No Me Dejes De Querer" won in the Best Video category at the Latin Grammys.) Just as the 1999 compilation album *20th Anniversary* had celebrated her veteran status in the music industry, so did 2001's

Greatest Hits, Vol. 2. This new disc contained a fresh remix of "Conga" supervised by the Estefans' son, Nayib. Also in 2001, Gloria and Emilio were inducted into the Songwriters Hall of Fame.

Speaking Out

Much as Gloria Estefan always wanted to avoid being caught in a political tug-of-war about Cuba, she could not stop herself from speaking out in 2000 when a controversial international incident occurred. Six-year-old Elian Gonzalez and his mother had fled from Cuba on a small craft, hoping to reach sanctuary in Miami. Along the way the boat sank and his mother drowned. The youngster survived, drifting on a life preserver until he was rescued. Brought to Florida to be with relatives, Elian's father— and the Cuban government—demanded his return to Cuba. Like many other Cuban Americans, Gloria felt strongly that the boy should remain in the U.S. To voice her beliefs she was among those who protested outside the house where the child was being kept. (Ultimately the boy was returned to Cuba.)

Earlier, in the late 1990s, Gloria had found herself in the midst of another political storm. Then she had spoken in defense of Peggi McKinley, who had been removed from the Miami-Dade County film board because she had criticized the group's ban on Cuban artists. Estefan was shocked that Americans were discriminating against Cubans, no matter what their political beliefs. When the singer wrote a letter to the editor of a Miami paper in defense of her point of view, the situation turned nasty. Her defense of equality for all was hotly debated in Miami newspapers, local radio stations, and especially among the city's large Cuban-American population. When some claimed that her attitude proved she was pro-communist, Gloria had to air her views in media interviews to set the record straight. On a far less controversial note, the singer performed at the closing ceremonies of the 2002 Winter Olympics at Salt Lake City, Utah. That September, Estefan was cohost of the annual Latin Grammys.

Back to Making Music

Reflecting her maturity as an artist and her zeal always to reach in new directions, Gloria offered a very personal artistic vision in the 2003 album *Unwrapped*. Her first English-language release in five years, *Unwrapped* showcased Gloria's contribution to all of the numbers, sometimes in collaboration with Jon Secada (e.g. "A Little Push"). Stevie Wonder teamed with the star on the cut "Into You," while singer Chrissie Hynde sang with Estefan on "One Name." This album avoided Gloria's past heavy emphasis on strong dance numbers. Instead, the new entry featured the singer's thoughts on life's tribulations, with occasional sidesteps into lighter tracks (e.g. "Te Amaré"). *Unwrapped* reached number 39 position on the *Billboard* Hot 200 (album) chart.

Also in 2003, Gloria was inducted into Florida's Women Hall of Fame and, in October gave seven performances at the massive Colosseum showroom at Caesar's Palace in Las Vegas.

As a major international star, Gloria continued to appear on a variety of English-language and Spanish-language talk shows, musical programs, and so forth. Occasionally, she popped up on TV sitcoms, such as when she guest-starred (as herself) on a February 2004 segment of the Showtime cable series *The Chris Isaak Show*. Then in April, she was a guest-judge for Latin music on an installment of TV's *American Idol*. Later in the month she claimed a prize in Miami at the Billboard Latin Music Awards for "Hoy," a single named Latin pop airplay track of the year.

Farewell Tour

In mid-2004, 46-year-old Gloria announced that in late July she would start what would be her farewell concert tour. She said, "Although I will continue writing and recording and doing everything else that comes with this incredible way of life, this next tour will be my last." She assured her fans that creating songs in the recording studio "never ceases to be a magical process for me." Estefan mentioned that she was also focusing on producing a feature film biography about singer Connie Francis. In addition, she said, "I have already started writing a 'book' in my head. Now I want to be able to put it on paper and communicate . . . on an even deeper level."

After several years of not touring in order to spend more time with her children, Estefan agreed to an exhaustive schedule for her farewell trek. The U.S. phase of the *Live and Re-wrapped Show* was a 27-city engagement, which began in Hidalgo, Texas, with stopovers in Atlanta, Boston, Chicago, Los Angeles, Philadelphia, and New York, and other cities, finishing in Miami in September 2004. This would be followed by an international tour covering Europe, Asia, and Latin America.

When the high-profile concert played at the Arrowhead Pond in Anaheim, California, Agustin Guerza (*Los Angeles Times*), observed of the veteran singer, "Her amazingly broad appeal was demonstrated by the all-inclusive demographics of Sunday's audience; old and young, bilingual and monolingual, white, black and Latino. . . . That global popularity, while forcing her music into a one-size-fits-all category, has made Estefan one of the most successful and enduring pop performers of her generation." Noting that Gloria had sold to date 70 million records worldwide, the reporter underscored, "Normally, sales alone don't mean much in an era of disposable pop.

But in the case of an immigrant Latina, it's a crucial accomplishment, because so few have been able to find mass acceptance in the U.S. She's the [Carlos] Santana of the East coast, and her fans admire her for that."

When the tour reached Illinois in late August 2004, Laura Emerick (*Chicago Sun-Times*) wrote of the superstar, "Her high spirits and good humor proved contagious as she charged from one segment to the next. There was disco Gloria . . . . There was contemplative Gloria. . . . But most of all, there was Gloria the consummate entertainer." Emerick reported, "Estefan celebrated her father . . . with a heart-tugging version of 'Cuando Sali de Cuba'—the first song she learned as a child. As Estefan accompanied herself on guitar, a tape of a 10-year-old Gloria singing that song to her soldier father came over the speakers; the effect was electrifying." During the course of the program at the United Center in Chicago, Gloria brought out on stage her daughter Emily, 10, who "did a mean Keith Moon imitation on the drums."

While Estefan was making her farewell concert tour, a new album (*Amor y Suerte: Exitos Romanticos*) was released in September 2004. It was a compilation of cuts from her past Spanish-language albums.

Facing the Future

In shaping her career as a major international recording artist, Gloria Estefan became a crossover talent, gaining

Gloria signs autographs for fans after a performance.
(Getty Images)

tremendous success in both Spanish and English-language marketplaces. She accomplished this tricky feat more than a decade before the "Latin explosion" of the late 1990s, which saw the rise of such artists as Ricky Martin, Jennifer Lopez, and Marc Anthony. Says Estefan, "In the [United] States, there's a kind of fear going on with music in another language, where in Europe and Latin America, two languages taught in school is a natural thing. It just makes for a broader experience. Maybe little by little the fear will go away and we'll be able to let in more sounds from different parts of the world."

One of Gloria's big dreams is one day to be able to perform in her homeland of Cuba. "That would be the only thing that could top any experience that I've had musically. Because no matter where I go, I'm not from there. . . . I have no sense of history other than what my parents have told me. I can't see where I was born. I cannot visit the place."

Although a long time has passed since the singer's nearly fatal bus accident in 1990, she can never truly forget that traumatic episode in her life. "But," says Gloria, "it's a wonderful reminder because it allows me, it reminds me, to live life to the fullest. . . . And I've always been very thankful for that." She notes that humor has "helped me through some very rough points. My humor can sometimes be irreverent, but every moment it has been there with me, even through the darkest moments. I think it

Gloria is committed to challenging herself in ways that encourage personal and professional growth. (WireImage)

helps us to not take ourselves too seriously. There is just too much to celebrate and too much to be grateful for."

On another occasion, the celebrated vocalist said, "I remember [as a youngster] having so many responsibilities trying to be strong for my mother, caring for my father. . . . that's why I'm determined to enjoy myself now. I've lived my life backwards in many ways."

With an estimated net worth of well over $200 million—from such enterprises as recordings, talent management, hotels, restaurants, music publishing, songwriting, as well as record, TV, and movie producing—the Estefans can well afford to live a luxuriant life without expanding their business empire. However, the star says they are driven to keep pushing at their commercial enterprises because "We still have the immigrant mentality and can never feel [financially] safe enough."

Gloria—whose remarkable career began in a modest Miami apartment, singing in the kitchen for her adoring grandmother—can only look ahead to many more professional challenges and experiments. In this she is guided by her belief, "There's no growth without a lot of hard work and a little risk. It's important to me that I continue to grow. There's no point in living life any other way."

TIME LINE

1957   Born Gloria Maria Milagrosa Fajardo in Havana, Cuba, on September 1, the first of two daughters

1959   Following revolutionary Fidel Castro's rise to power in Cuba, the Fajardos leave the island for life in Miami, Florida

1961   Father (José Manuel Fajardo) is taken prisoner in the failed invasion of Cuba at the Bay of Pigs; he remains jailed in Cuba until late 1962

1963   Father, having joined the U.S. Army, is stationed to military bases in Texas and, later, in South Carolina, with his family accompanying him

1966   Receives a guitar for her ninth birthday

1975   Graduates from Our Lady of Lourdes Academy and enters University of Miami; meets rising musician/ entrepreneur Emilio Estefan Jr. and begins singing with his group, Miami Latin Boys (soon renamed Miami Sound Machine)

1977   Miami Sound Machine (MSM) records debut album (*Renacer*) on independent Audio Latino label

1978   Receives B.A. from University of Miami; marries Emilio Estefan Jr. in Miami; album: *Miami Sound Machine* (independent)

1979   Album: *Imported* (independent)

1980   MSM signs recording contract with Discos CBS International, with *MSM* their first album for new label; group continues to tour Central and South America; son Nayib born; father dies

1981   Album: *Otra Vez* (Discos CBS International)

1982   Album: *Rio* (Discos CBS International)

1983   Album: *Lo Mejor de Miami Sound Machine* (Discos CBS International)

1984   With release of English-language song "Dr. Beat," MSM has a huge crossover hit in the U.S., leading to band switching to Epic Records; albums: *A Toda Máquina* (Discos CBS International), *Eyes of Innocence* (Epic)

1985   MSM's single, "Conga," makes industry history by being first song to appear on four different music pop charts simultaneously; album: *Primitive Love* (Epic)

1986   Appears in ABC-TV movie *Club Med*

1987   Makes first music video; to support new album release, the band (now known as Gloria Estefan and Miami Sound Machine) go on world tour; the Estefans purchase Star Island home on Miami's Biscayne Bay; album: *Let It Loose* (Epic)

1988   Band has number-one pop hit with "Anything for You"; Gloria and MSM win an American Music Award

1989   By now she is the solo artist for her band and the only remaining original member of MSM; album: *Cuts Both Ways* (Epic)

1990   Performs at American Music Awards and the Grammys; band given the Crystal Globe Award; the Estefans meet with President George Bush at White House; Gloria's back severely injured in bus accident; album: *Exitos de Gloria Estefan* (Epic—compilation disc)

1991   Making a full recovery, Gloria back on stage/tour with MSM in support of latest disc, with "Coming

Out of the Dark"—another number one hit on pop charts; album: *Into the Light* (Epic)

1992 Album: *Greatest Hits* (Epic—compilation disc)

1993 New disc *Mi Tierra* (Epic) earns Grammy Award

1994 Birth of daughter Emily; album: *Hold Me, Thrill Me, Kiss Me* (Epic)

1995 Performs concert at U.S. naval base in Guantánamo, Cuba; wet bike crashes into Estefans' motor boat, killing the driver; album: *Abriendo Puertas* (Epic) earns Grammy Award; album: *Christmas through Your Eyes* (Epic)

1996 Sings at closing ceremony of Olympics in Atlanta, Georgia; embarks on world tour; HBO cable special *Gloria Estefan: The Evolution Tour—Live in Miami* wins NCLR Bravo Award; album: *Destiny* (Epic)

1998 Participates in VH1 cable's *Divas Live* concert; album: *gloria!* (Epic)

1999 Nominated for Lifetime Achievement Award from the ALMA Awards; makes feature film debut in *Music of the Heart* (Miramax); album: *20th Anniversary* (Epic—compilation)

2000 Album *Alma Caribeña* (Epic) wins Grammy; becomes embroiled in political controversy regarding six-year-old Cuban refugee Elian Gonzalez; wins Award of Merit at American Music Awards; other albums: *Greatest Hits* (Epic—compilation); TV movie: *For Love of Country: The Arturo Sandoval Story* (HBO)

2001 Gloria and Emilio Estefan Jr. are inducted into the Songwriters Hall of Fame; album: *Greatest Hits, Vol. 2* (Epic—compilation)

2002 Performs at Winter Olympics at Salt Lake City, Utah

2003 Performs at Caesar's Palace in Las Vegas; inducted into Florida's Women Hall of Fame; album: *Unwrapped* (Epic)

2004 Begins farewell tour in U.S. with later playdates in Europe, Asia, and Central/South America; album: *Amor y Suerte: Exitos Romanticos* (Epic—compilation)

HOW TO BECOME A SINGER

THE JOB

Singers are employed to perform music with their voices by using their knowledge of vocal sound and delivery, harmony, melody, and rhythm. They put their individual vocal styles into the songs they sing, and they interpret music accordingly. The sounds of the voices in a performance play a significant part in how a song will affect an audience; this essential aspect of a singer's voice is known as its tone.

Classical singers are usually categorized according to the range and quality of their voices, beginning with the highest singing voice, the soprano, and ending with the lowest, the bass; voices in between include mezzo soprano, contralto, tenor, and baritone. Singers perform either alone (in which case they are referred to as soloists) or as members of an ensemble, or group. They sing by either following a score, which is the printed musical text, or by memorizing the material. Also, they may sing either with or without instrumental accompaniment; singing without accompaniment is called a cappella. In opera—which are plays set to music—singers perform the various roles, much as actors do, interpreting the drama with their voice to the accompaniment of a symphony orchestra.

Classical singers may perform a variety of musical styles, or specialize in a specific period; they may give recitals, or perform as members of an ensemble. Classical singers generally undergo years of voice training and instruction in musical theory. They develop their vocal technique and learn how to project without harming their voices. Classical singers rarely use a microphone when they sing; nonetheless, their voices must be heard above the orchestra. Because classical singers often perform music from many different languages, they learn how to pronounce these languages, and often how to speak them as well. Those who are involved in opera work for opera companies in major cities throughout the country and often travel extensively. Some classical singers also perform in other musical areas.

Professional singers tend to perform in a chosen style of music, such as jazz, rock, or blues, among many others.

Many singers pursue careers that will lead them to perform for coveted recording contracts, on concert tours, and for television and motion pictures. Others perform in rock, pop, country, gospel, or folk groups, singing in venues such as concert halls, nightclubs, and churches and at social gatherings and for small studio recordings. Whereas virtuosos, classical artists who are expertly skilled in their singing style, tend to perform traditional pieces that have been handed down through hundreds of years, singers in other areas often perform popular, current pieces, and often songs that they themselves have composed.

Another style of music in which formal training is often helpful is jazz. Jazz singers learn phrasing, breathing, and vocal techniques; often, the goal of a jazz singer is to become as much a part of the instrumentation as the piano, saxophone, trumpet, or trombone. Many jazz singers perform "scat" singing, in which the voice is used in an improvisational way much like another instrument.

Folk singers perform songs that may be many years old, or they may write their own songs. Folk singers generally perform songs that express a certain cultural tradition; while some folk singers specialize in their own or another culture, others may sing songs from a great variety of cultural and musical traditions. In the United States, folk singing is particularly linked to the acoustic guitar, and many singers accompany themselves while singing.

A cappella singing, which is singing without musical accompaniment, takes many forms. A cappella music may be a part of classical music; it may also be a part of folk music, as in the singing of barbershop quartets. Another form, called doo-wop, is closely linked to rock and rhythm-and-blues music.

Gospel music, which evolved in the United States, is a form of sacred music; gospel singers generally sing as part of a choir, accompanied by an organ, or other musical instruments, but may also perform a cappella. Many popular singers began their careers as singers in church and gospel choirs before entering jazz, pop, blues, or rock.

Pop/rock singers generally require no formal training whatsoever. Rock music is a very broad term encompassing many different styles of music, such as heavy metal, punk, rap, rhythm and blues, rockabilly, techno, and many others. Rock singers learn to express themselves and their music, developing their own phrasing and vocal techniques. Rock singers usually sing as part of a band, or with a backing band to accompany them. Rock singers usually sing with microphones so that they can be heard above the amplified instruments around them.

All singers practice and rehearse their songs and music. Some singers read from music scores while performing; others perform from memory. Yet all must gain an intimate knowledge of their music, so that they can best convey its meanings and feelings to their audience. Singers must also exercise their voices even when not performing. Some singers perform as featured soloists and artists. Others perform as part of a choir, or as backup singers adding harmony to the lead singer's voice.

REQUIREMENTS
High School

Many singers require no formal training in order to sing. However, those interested in becoming classical or jazz singers should begin learning and honing their talent when they are quite young. Vocal talent can be recognized in grade school students and even in younger children. In general, however, these early years are a time of vast development and growth in singing ability. Evident changes occur in boys' and girls' voices when they are around 12 to 14 years old, during which time their vocal cords go through a process of lengthening and thickening. Boys' voices tend to change much more so than girls' voices, although both genders should be provided with challenges that will help them achieve their creative goals. Young students should learn about breath control and why it is necessary; they should learn to follow a conductor, including the relationship between hand and baton motions and the dynamics of the music; and they should learn about musical concepts such as tone, melody, harmony, and rhythm.

During the last two years of high school, aspiring singers should have a good idea of what classification they are in, according to the range and quality of their voices: soprano, alto, contralto, tenor, baritone, or bass. These categories indicate the resonance of the voice; soprano being the highest and lightest, bass being the lowest and heaviest. Students should take part in voice classes, choirs, and ensembles. In addition, students should continue their studies in English, writing, social studies, foreign language, and other electives in music, theory, and performance.

There tend to be no formal educational requirements for those who wish to be singers. However, formal education is valuable, especially in younger years. Some students know early in their lives that they want to be singers and are ambitious enough to continually practice and learn. These students are often advised to attend high schools that are specifically geared toward combined academic and intensive arts education in music, dance, and theater. Such schools can provide valuable preparation and guidance for those who plan to pursue professional careers in the arts. Admission is usually based on results from students' auditions as well as academic testing.

Postsecondary Training

Many find it worthwhile and fascinating to continue their study of music and voice in a liberal arts program at a college or university. Similarly, others attend schools of higher education that are focused specifically on music, such as the Juilliard School (http://www.juilliard.edu) in New York. Such an intense program would include a multidisciplinary curriculum of composition and performance, as well as study of the history, development, variety, and potential advances of music. In this type of program, a student would earn a bachelor of arts degree. To earn a bachelor of science degree in music, one would study musicology, which concerns the history, literature, and cultural background of music; the music industry, which will prepare one for not only singing but also marketing music and other business aspects; and professional performance. Specific music classes in a typical four-year liberal arts program would include such courses as introduction to music, music styles and structures, harmony, theory of music, elementary and advanced auditory training, music history, and individual instruction.

In addition to learning at schools, many singers are taught by private singing teachers and voice coaches, who help to develop and refine students' voices. Many aspiring singers take courses at continuing adult education centers, where they can take advantage of courses in beginning and advanced singing, basic vocal techniques, voice coaching, and vocal performance workshops. When one is involved in voice training, he or she must learn about good articulation and breath control, which are very important qualities for all singers. Performers must take care of their voices and keep their lungs in good condition. Voice training, whether as part of a college curriculum or in private study, is useful to many singers, not only for classical and opera singers, but also for jazz singers and for those interested in careers in musical theater. Many singers who have already achieved professional success continue to take voice lessons throughout their careers.

Other Requirements

In other areas of music, learning to sing and becoming a singer is often a matter of desire, practice, and an inborn love and talent for singing. Learning to play a musical instrument is often extremely helpful, as is developing one's ability to sing and to read and write music. Sometimes it is not even necessary to have a "good" singing voice. Many singers in rock music have less-than-perfect voices, and rap artists generally do not really sing at all. But these singers learn to use their voices in ways that nonetheless provide good expression to their songs, music, and ideas.

EXPLORING

Anyone who is interested in pursuing a career as a singer should obviously have a love for music. Listen to recordings as often as possible, and get an understanding of the types of music that you enjoy. Singing, alone or with family and friends, is one of the most natural ways to explore music and develop a sense of your own vocal style. Join music clubs at school, as well as the school band if it does vocal performances. In addition, take part in school drama productions that involve musical numbers.

Older students interested in classical music careers could contact trade associations such as the American Guild of Musical Artists, as well as read trade journals such as *Hot Line News* (published by Musicians National Hot Line Association), which covers news about singers and other types of musicians and their employment needs and opportunities. For information and news about very popular singers, read *Billboard* magazine (http://www.billboard.com), which can be purchased at many local bookshops and newsstands. Those who already know what type of music they wish to sing should audition for roles in community musical productions or contact trade groups that offer competitions. For example, the Central Opera Service (Metropolitan Opera, Lincoln Center, New York, NY 10023) can provide information on competitions, apprentice programs, and performances for young singers interested in opera.

There are many summer programs offered throughout the United States for high school students interested in singing and other performing arts. For example, Stanford University offers its Stanford Jazz Workshop each summer for students who are at least 12 years old. It offers activities in instrumental and vocal music. For college students who are 18 years and older, the jazz workshop has a number of positions available.

Another educational institute that presents a summer program is Boston University's Tanglewood Institute, which is geared especially toward very talented and ambitious students between the ages of 15 and 18. It offers sessions in chorus, musical productions, chamber music, classical music, ensemble, instrumental, and vocal practice. Arts and culture field trips are also planned. College students who are at least 20 years old can apply for available jobs at the summer Tanglewood programs.

Students interested in other areas of singing can begin while still in high school, or even sooner. Many gospel singers, for example, start singing with their local church group at an early age. Many high school students form their own bands, playing rock, country, or jazz, and can gain experience performing before an audience; some of these young musicians even get paid to perform at school parties and other social functions.

EMPLOYERS

There are many different environments in which singers can be employed, including lounges, bars cafes, radio and television, theater productions, cruise ships, resorts, hotels, casinos, large concert tours, and opera companies.

Many singers hire agents, who usually receive a percentage of the singer's earnings for finding them appropriate performance contracts. Others are employed primarily as *studio singers,* which means that they do not perform for live audiences but rather record their singing in studios for albums, radio, television, and motion pictures.

An important tactic for finding employment as a singer is to invest in a professional-quality recording of your singing that you can send to prospective employers.

STARTING OUT

There is no single correct way to enter the singing profession. It is recommended that aspiring singers explore the avenues that interest them, continuing to apply and audition for whatever medium suits them. Singing is an extremely creative profession, and singers must learn to be creative and resourceful in the business matters of finding opportunities to perform.

High school students should seek out any performance opportunities, including choirs, school musical productions, and church and other religious functions. Singing teachers can arrange recitals and introduce students to their network of musician contacts.

ADVANCEMENT

In the singing profession and the music industry in general, the nature of the business is such that singers can consider themselves to have "made it" when they get steady, full-time work. A measure of advancement is how well known and respected singers become in their field, which in turn influences their earnings. In most areas, particularly classical music, only the most talented and persistent singers make it to the top of their profession. In other areas, success may be largely a matter of luck and perseverance.

Also, many experienced singers who have had formal training will become voice teachers. Reputable schools such as Juilliard consider it a plus when a student can say that he or she has studied with a master.

EARNINGS

As with many occupations in the performing arts, earnings for singers are highly dependent on one's professional reputation and thus cover a wide range. To some degree, pay is also related to educational background (as it relates to how well one has been trained) and geographic location of performances. In certain situations, such as singing for audio recordings, pay is dependent on the number of minutes of finished music (for instance, an hour's pay will be given for each three and a half minutes of recorded song).

Singing is often considered a glamorous occupation. However, because it attracts so many professionals, competition for positions is very high. Only a small proportion of those who aspire to be singers achieve glamorous jobs and extremely lucrative contracts. Famous opera singers, for example earn $8,000 and more for each performance. Singers in an opera chorus earn between $600 and $800 per week. Classical soloists can receive between $2,000 and $3,000 per performance, while choristers may receive around $70 per performance. For rock singers, earnings can be far higher. Within the overall group of professional singers, studio and opera singers tend to earn salaries that are well respected in the industry; their opportunities for steady, long-term contracts tend to be better than for singers in other areas.

Average salaries for musicians, singers, and related workers were $37,120 in 2004, according to the U.S. Department of Labor. The lowest-paid 10 percent earned less than $13,458 per year, while the highest-paid 10 percent earned more than $111,000 annually.

Top studio and opera singers earn an average of $70,000 per year, though some earn much more. Rock singers may begin by playing for drinks and meals only; if successful, they may earn tens of thousands of dollars for a single performance. Singers on cruise ships generally earn between $750 and $2,000 per week, although these figures can vary considerably. Also, many singers supplement their performance earnings by working at other positions, such as teaching at schools or giving private lessons or even working at jobs unrelated to singing. The U.S. Department of Labor reports that median salaries in 2004 for full-time teachers were as follows: elementary, $43,160; middle school, $43,670; and high school, $45,650.

Because singers rarely work for a single employer, they generally receive no fringe benefits, and must provide their own health insurance and retirement planning.

WORK ENVIRONMENT

The environments in which singers work tend to vary greatly, depending on such factors as type of music involved and location of performance area. Professional singers often work in the evenings and during weekends, and many are frequently required to travel. Many singers who are involved in popular productions such as in opera, rock, and country music work in large cities such as New York, Las Vegas, Chicago, Los Angeles, and Nashville. Stamina and endurance are needed to keep up with the hours of rehearsals and performances, which can be long; work schedules are very often erratic, varying from job to job.

Many singers are members of trade unions, which represent them in matters such as wage scales and fair working conditions. Vocal performers who sing for studio recordings are represented by the American Federation of Television and Radio Artists; solo opera singers, solo concert singers, and choral singers are members of the American Guild of Musical Artists.

OUTLOOK

According to the U.S. Department of Labor, employment for singers, as for musicians in general, is expected to grow about as fast as the average for all other occupations through 2012. The entertainment industry is expected to grow during the next decade, which will create jobs for singers and other performers.

TO LEARN MORE ABOUT SINGERS

BOOKS

Alderson, Richard. *The Complete Book of Voice Training.* Grand Rapids, Mich.: Parker, 1979.

Baugeuss, David. *Sight Singing Made Simple.* Milwaukee, Wisc.: Hal Leonard, 1995.

Brow, Oren L. *Discover Your Voice: How to Develop Healthy Voice Habits.* Clifton Park, N.Y.: Singular, 1996.

Emmons, Shirlee, and Alma Thomas. *Power Performance for Singers: Transcending the Barriers.* New York: Oxford University Press, 1998.

Sutherland, Susan. *Teach Yourself Singing.* New York: McGraw-Hill, 1996.

ORGANIZATIONS AND WEBSITES

For information on membership in a local union nearest you, developments in the music field, a searchable database of U.S. and foreign music schools, and articles on careers in music, visit the following website.

American Federation of Musicians of the United States and Canada

1501 Broadway, Suite 600

New York, NY 10036

Tel: 212-869-1330

http://www.afm.org

The AGMA is a union for professional musicians. The website has information on upcoming auditions, news announcements for the field, and membership information.

American Guild of Musical Artists (AGMA)

1430 Broadway, 14th Floor

New York, NY 10018

Tel: 212-265-3687

Email: AGMA@MusicalArtists.org

http://www.musicalartists.org

For more information on *Hot Line News,* contact

Musicians National Hot Line Association

277 East 6100 South
Salt Lake City, UT 84107
Tel: 801-268-2000

For a list of colleges and universities that offer music-related programs, contact
National Association of Schools of Music
11250 Roger Bacon Drive, Suite 21
Reston, VA 20190
Tel: 703-437-0700
Email: info@arts-accredit.org
http://nasm.arts-accredit.org

For career and educational information for opera singers, contact
Opera America
1156 15th Street, Suite 810
Washington, DC 20005
Tel: 202-293-4466
Email: Frontdesk@operaamerica.org
http://www.operaam.org

For information on music programs, contact the following:
Boston University, Tanglewood Institute
855 Commonwealth Avenue

Boston, MA 02215
http://www.bu.edu/cfa/music/tanglewood

Stanford University, Jazz Workshop

Box 20454

Stanford, CA 94309

Tel: 650-736-0324

Email: info@stanfordjazz.org

http://www.stanfordjazz.org

TO LEARN MORE ABOUT GLORIA ESTEFAN

BOOKS

Backbeat. *Definitive Guide to Rock, Pop, and Soul.* 3d ed. San Francisco: Backbeat, 2002.

Benson, Michael. *Gloria Estefan.* Minneapolis: Lerner, 2000.

Bogdanov, Vladimir, Chris Woodstra, and Stephen Thomas Erlewine, eds. *All Music Guide to Rock: The Definitive Guide to Rock, Pop, and Soul.* 3d ed. San Francisco: Backbeat, 2002.

Boulais, Sue. *Gloria Estefan.* Childs, Md.: Mitchell Lane, 1998.*

Bronson, Fred. _The Billboard Book of Number One Hits_ (5th ed). New York: Billboard/Watson-Guptill, 2003.

Catalano, Grace. _Gloria Estefan_. New York: St Martin's, 1991.

DeStefano, Anthony M. _Gloria Estefan: The Pop Superstar From Tragedy to Triumph_. New York: Signet, 1997.

Editors. _1995 Current Biography Yearbook_. Bronx, N.Y.: H. W. Wilson, 1995.

Gonzales, Doreen. _Gloria Estefan: Singer and Entertainer_. Springfield, N.J.: Enslow, 1998.*

Gonzalez, Fernando. _Gloria Estefan: Cuban-American Singing Star_. New York: Millbrook, 1993.*

Gourse, Leslie. _Gloria Estefan: Pop Sensation_. London, England: Franklin Watts, 2000.*

Henderson, Ashyia N., ed. _Contemporary Hispanic Biography,_ Vol. 1. Farmington Hills, Mich.: Gale, 2002.

Kramer, Barbara. _Gloria Estefan: Never Give Up_. Springfield, N.J.: Enslow, 2004.*

Nielson, Shelly. _Gloria Estefan: International Pop Star_. Minneapolis: Abdo & Daughters, 1993.*

Parish, James Robert, and Allan Taylor: _The Encyclopedia of Ethnic Groups in Hollywood_. New York: Facts on File, 2002.

Phillips, Jane. _Gloria Estefan_. Philadelphia: Chelsea House, 2001.*

Riggs, Thomas, ed. _Contemporary Theatre, Film and Television_, Vol. 40. Farmington Hills, Mich.: Gale, 2002.

Rodriguez, Janel. *Gloria Estefan.* New York: Steck-Vaughn/Harcourt, 1995.*

Romanowski, Patricia, Holly George-Warren, and John Pareles, eds. *The Rolling Stone Encyclopedia of Rock & Roll.* 3d ed. New York: Fireside, 2001.

Shirley, David. *Gloria Estefan. Queen of Latin Pop.* Philadelphia: Chelsea Juniors/Chelsea House, 1994.*

Stefoff, Rebecca. *Gloria Estefan.* Philadelphia: Chelsea House, 1991.*

Strazzabosco, Jeanne. *Learning About Determination from the Life of Gloria Estefan.* New York: PowerKids/Rosen Publishing, 1996.*

* Young Adult Book

WEBSITES

AllMusic

http://www.allmusic.com

E! Online

http://www.eonline.com

Gloria Estefan

http://users.skynet.be/gloriaestefan/destinyhome.html

Gloria Estefan

http://www.epiccenter.com/EpicCenter/custom/56/flash.htm

Gloria Estefan Discography
http://www.gloriadiscography.net

Gloria Estefan Library
http://members.v3space.com/gloriaestefanlibrary

Gloria Estefan: Miami Spice
http://www.angelfire.com/nj/miamispice/MiamiSpice.html

Gloria Estefan Official Fan Site
http://www.gloriaestefan.com

Gloria Estefan Shrine
http://members.tripod.com/~felicidad/index.html

Gloria Estefan UK Fan Club
http://www.gloria.ndirect.co.uk

Gloria Heaven
http://www.gloriaheaven.com

Gloria Time
http://www.angelfire.com/sc2/gloriatime/frames.html

Internet Movie Database
http://www.imdb.com

Rock on the Net

http://www.rockonthenet.com

Sony Music

http://sonymusic.com

VH1

http://www.vh1.com

INDEX

Page numbers in *italics* indicate illustrations.

A

Abriendo Puertas [Opening Doors] (record album and song) 70, 72, 79

Alma Caribeña [Caribbean Soul] (record album) 30, 78

"Along Came You (A Song for Emily)" (song) 73

"Always Tomorrow" (song) 66

American Idol (television series) 81

Amor y Suerte: Exitos Romanticos (record album) 83

Anthony, Marc 85

Any Given Sunday (film) 77

"Anything for You" (song) 48–49

A Toda Máquina [At Full Speed] (record album) 38

Avila, Juan Marcos 24, *41,* 44–45

B

"Bad Boy" (song) 44–45, 56

Batista, General Fulgencio 8–10

Bay of Pigs Invasion of Cuba 11–12, *13*

"Breaking Up Is Hard to Do" (song) 68

Bush, George H. W. (President) 1, 56, *57*

C

Carey, Mariah 75

Carpenter, Karen 19

Casas, Jorge 53

Castro, Fidel 9–12, 22, 29, 34–35, 51, 70, 74

The Chris Isaak Show (television series) 81

Christmas Through Your Eyes (record album and song) 70

ABOUT THE AUTHOR

James Robert Parish, a former entertainment reporter, publicist, and book series editor, is the author of numerous biographies and reference books of the entertainment industry including *Jennifer Lopez: Actor; Katie Couric: TV Newscaster; Stan Lee: Comic-Book Writer; Twyla Tharp: Choreographer; Denzel Washington: Actor; Halle Berry: Actor; Stephen King: Writer; Tom Hanks: Actor; Steven Spielberg: Filmmaker; Fiasco: A History of Hollywood's Iconic Flops; Katharine Hepburn: The Untold Story; The Hollywood Book of Scandal; Whitney Houston; The Hollywood Book of Love; Hollywood Divas; Hollywood Bad Boys; The Encyclopedia of Ethnic Groups in Hollywood; Jet Li; Gus Van Sant; The Hollywood Book of Death; Whoopi Goldberg; Rosie O'Donnell's Story; The Unofficial "Murder, She Wrote" Casebook; Today's Black Hollywood;* and *Let's Talk! America's Favorite TV Talk Show Hosts.*

Mr. Parish is a frequent on-camera interviewee on cable and network TV for documentaries on the performing arts both in the United States and in the United Kingdom. Mr. Parish resides in Studio City, California. His website is http://www.jamesrobertparish.com.